OUR COMMON NEUROSIS

Our Common Neurosis

Notes on a Group Experiment

CHARLES B. THOMPSON, M.D.
and
ALFREDA P. SILL

With fifty-three sketches and essays by
members of a research group, used to
illustrate and explain a fresh approach
to problems of human relations

Foreword by Trigant Burrow, M.D., Ph.D.

EXPOSITION PRESS • NEW YORK

Foreword

Dr. Thompson's request that I write a foreword to this small volume of essays and stories that silhouette, as it were, some of the commoner problems in human behavior invites a backward glance to the early years of my psychoanalytic practice and research. For the writings gathered here grew out of an experimental innovation that marked my first researches in group- or phylo-analysis. As I look back over the years of my psychiatric experience, I cannot but be impressed by the great change in attitude and outlook that has been wrought in the brief life-span of a single generation. I gratefully recall that it was the early intimations of Freud's original work in psycho-analysis, as it began to seep into this country during the first decade of the century, that gave fresh impetus and direction to what proved for me a lifelong study of human behavior. The dynamic formulations of Freud gave rhyme and reason to nervous and mental disorders. Through the impact of his teaching, habitual preoccupation with the dry, classificatory listing of bizarre symptoms and syndromes gave way to an intimate understanding of the meaning of these clinical appearances within the distorted personality blindly fighting against unconscious odds in his quest for adjustment and expression. Emphasis was suddenly shifted from the "what" to the "why" of behavior aberrations. The emotionally confused patient was no longer consigned to the deadening routine of institutional care, but was restored to the warmth of sympathy and understanding so essential to the rehabilitation of the socially exiled mind.

As great and revolutionary, however, as was Freud's contribution to the interpretation and treatment of mental and emotional imbalances, it seemed to me even in my early days of psychoanalytic practice that an important factor was missing, that Freud's investigations were lacking in sociobiological breadth. What were the community implications in the symptomatology of the neurotic or psychotic patient? What about the social milieu in which these untoward behavior expressions had their inception and perpetuation? Were not the mechanisms of repression, projection, self-deception, narcism, and kindred expressions characteristic of the larger social community as well? Were not the symptoms we viewed with such clarity and objectivity in our patients also present, if in seemingly less bizarre, less painful form, in human society generally? Was it true that our so-called "normal" interrelational behavior represented the desired goal? Did "normality" really embody a stable and dependable criterion? Was it physiologically sound, biologically determined, sociologically oriented? In short, was it free, balanced, wholesome? Or did it merely represent behavior that was participated in by the majority of individuals and endorsed by the prevailing social system?

In the larger view, did not the standard of normality include within its scope personalities who were individually as disparate, socially as secretive and egocentric, as the isolated patient with his more arresting, more dramatic reaction? If this was so, psychiatry was hardly scientific in looking only at the evidences of disordered behavior in the individual patient and attempting to restore him to the behavior norm habitual to the wider community—the very medium in which his symptoms had their inception and development. Perhaps, I thought, a more basic approach was to be found in the study of the social group, which is composed of both normal and

neurotic personalities—the group or community in which the
unconscious processes of both "neurotic" and "normal" are
equally nourished. Was it not to be found in the analysis of
the *self* as an *organismic social unit* within the social setting
of other selves? After all, regardless of the popular emphasis
on "rugged individualism," man is a social animal. The data
of biology, sociology, and anthropology give unequivocal support to this fact. Hence the behavior of the individual cannot
be adequately evaluated apart from that of his interacting
group. It seemed to me, therefore, that if we were to follow
the course of science, and discover the common denominator
in our human pathology—a pathology that characterizes the
behavior of the "normal" community as well as of the
"neurotic" patient—it was essential that our immediate social
groups become the subject of intensive study and research.

Such considerations indicate something of the background
of thinking and feeling that gave rise to my first venture in
group analysis, a venture which was initiated when, in the
interest of experimentation, I invited a student of particularly
keen insight and capacity to interchange roles with me. And
so, the student, for many years now my distinguished associate,
Mr. Clarence Shields, assumed the function of the analyst and
I, in turn, became the analysand. This phase, while offering
new insights and affording interesting material in regard to
the arbitrary absolutism, the false organization of the "self,"
soon outlived its usefulness. But I was now more than ever
convinced that only in some form of community or group
analysis was there to be found the key to the conflict in behavior that not only plagued the neurotic personality but that
was also apparent within so-called normal interrelationships.
These "normal" interrelationships are characterized throughout by emotional instability, sexual obsessions, phrenetic competitiveness, feelings of anxiety and insecurity, economic

imbalance entailing inequalities of opportunity—in short, by aberrations in social feeling and thinking that inevitably lead to insanity, crime, and war. As a consequence, I invited others of my experienced students and patients to participate in our social experiment. Needless to say, such an innovation was in those days regarded as eminently unconventional and, as might be expected, the great majority of my psychoanalytic colleagues looked with ill-concealed disfavor upon my highly unorthodox investigations.

Today, group procedures in psychotherapy are of course a commonplace. A recent survey of the field listed references to more than two hundred reported group-studies. I should emphasize, however, the basic differences between these later therapeutic methods and the pioneer analytic inquiries of my associates and myself. In the studies conducted by our professional group, no conventionally established distinction was made between physician and patient. Physician and patient alike were placed in the common position of investigators of a community behavior disorder that affected them both equally. Our group-analytic sessions were primarily oriented in the direction of research, not of therapy. However much we may have fumbled at first, our objectives were consistently pursued. In these objectives we sought to arrest within ourselves, in the immediate moment and in the immediate social setting, *the projection of interpersonal affect or prejudice*, and to discover, if possible, the internal physiological displacement involved in man's habitual tendency to affect-projection.

It was our aim to demarcate between an organismically congruent and an organismically disjunctive pattern of tension. Our purpose was not to look at the *symptoms* of behavior, either in oneself or in the other person, but to study the underlying causes of behavior that were basic and common to us both. As I have elsewhere said: "In my group work there has not been at any time the attempt to show what human behavior ought or ought not to be, but rather to show how human behavior has been artificially deflected from what it primarily, biologically *is*. Our work has consisted largely in the effort to define a *mood* we definitely recognized in the reactions of the individual and of social groups as being arbitrary and unstable, and to see that man is now adamant in his resistance to the recognition of this arbitrary mood as a falsely imbued sense of the 'self.' We set out, associates, students, and I, to study our *selves*—the *social self* of man and his motivations as a species."

In these brief essays and stories that Dr. Thompson and Mrs. Sill have assembled, the reader will not find unrivaled examples of flawless literary style, nor will he be impressed with their profound philosophical reflections or .with their penetrating scientific insights and discoveries. The interest of this gathered material lies in its sociopsychiatric implications. It represents in a sense a glimpse into the first sociobiological clinic. In our early group experiments, in our initial examination of cross-sections of the social community, we had of course not yet attained the level of a phylobiological laboratory. But here were people, each of whom was banked off from the others in the isolation of his own private neurosis. Each had felt keenly the pain of his self-inflicted ostracism from the social community, yet each had felt no less the complemental satisfaction of his wishfully achieved encystment. In this poignant arrest of interest and productivity, theirs was the impasse of dichotomy and conflict. But, with the very first opportunity for cooperation in a group endeavor unsponsored by precept or authority, something unexpected happened. These ill-adjusted personalities were suddenly alerted to the interest of consensual activity.

In this phase of my efforts to correlate the knotty problem of individual neurosis with social disorders and conflict, the concept of the solidarity of man as a species had not become clear to me in any definite biological terms. My associates and I had not as yet undertaken the physiological experiments that later verified the generic nature of neurosis, or the dissociation expressed in the vaunted "normality" of social man. The existence of the falsely organized sense of the self, or the "I"-persona, as I now call it, and the domination of mankind by this insidious, autocratic mood, had not yet been experimentally demonstrated as a proved biological fact. Furthermore, we were still to wait years before the differentiation between two physiologically conflicting patterns of tension internal to the organism could be objectively demonstrated by us. As later writings of my associates and myself have shown, these researches indicate a fundamental difference in tensional patterns of vital significance in man's adaptation to the environment. One of these patterns corresponds to the behavior biologically normal to man as a species, the other to the behavior of man when subjected to the artificial dictates of the social "I"-complex or "I"-persona.

At that time I had not described in the exact experimental terms of the laboratory the difference between a fanciful, personal "right" such as is universally inculcated by the older generation in the younger, and the basic, organic right determining the behavior of man as a unitary species. The discrimination between the physiological pattern of behavior that corresponds to man's biologically normal right on the one hand, and the internal pattern of behavior that is coincident with the fanciful or wishful "right" of his pseudonormality on the other, is today the very core of our phylobiological position.*

And so, the essays here collected under the title, *Our Common Neurosis*, embrace a period that marks only the rudimentary beginnings of our later laboratory experimentation. Throughout these essays the discerning reader cannot fail to detect in the unilateral mood of the writers the same artificial assumption of autocratic "rightness" proved by subsequent investigations to be the underlying factor in the abnormal isolation and separation of both individuals and communities. Thus our vignettes really provide samples of much inept, adolescent thinking. They exemplify the very symptoms which their authors were supposedly observing. In short, the writings are themselves largely expressions of our so-called normality. Such is the dilemma of the social neurosis in both lay and professional groups. It is only too plain, therefore, that in their valiant attempts to elucidate the symptoms of a common neurosis these anonymous neurotics have unwittingly disclosed clinical evidence of the very neurosis they themselves have essayed to set forth. But thereby hangs a tale—a tale which our wider communities would do well to take to heart if they are interested in recognizing the involvement of themselves and their children in a world-wide social neurosis.

But this was long ago. Much water has flowed under the bridge since these early years of our group analysis. It was from the background of these first years of group association that the sketches contained in this small volume emerged. Thus the writings and the group analysis represent parallel

---

* The reader is referred to Dr. Burrow's paper, "Emotion and the Social Crisis: A Problem in Phylobiology," published in *Feelings and Emotions: The Mooseheart Symposium* (New York: McGraw-Hill Book Co., 1950), pp. 465–86.—EDITORS.

expressions in the course of a unique endeavor in social integration—an endeavor that resulted in a distinctly altered frame of reference for the study and understanding of human behavior and its disorders. In their accompanying comments, the editors have attempted to observe this material from the point of view of the later phases of our group researches. I am the more glad that these vignettes are being published in book form since I feel that they may be of some small assistance to those present-day groups in this country and elsewhere which have, on their own initiative, undertaken studies patterned along our phyloanalytic lines.

In the slow progression from myth to matter, in the gradual replacement of magic with medicine, the evolution of man has been both dramatic and consistent. But this process in the integration of man's behavior has today been suddenly brought up against a more immediate, a more urgent developmental necessity. Man must now shift from the projective palliatives of fantasy and wish to the concrete recognition within himself of a tangible contrast in patterns of tension. Only with such a radical behavior-adjustment throughout the species shall we be able to meet the rapidly oncoming social crisis of discord and disintegration that now threatens the very survival of man.

As I have said, there has been a marked change in the psychiatric climate since the initiation of our phyloanalytic work. The social nature of behavior disorders is accepted today, at least theoretically. Moreover, the current estimate of the importance of the physiological substrate of nervous and mental disorders is amply demonstrated by the wide therapeutic use of the various shock treatments, of prefrontal brain-operations, and by the emphasis on psychosomatic medicine. It has become a commonplace to speak, ho   ~ academically, of "tensions" in regard to the behavior of   dividual, and one of the important projects of UNESCO is the study of "Tensions Affecting International Understanding." While it is a far cry from these symbolically conceived tensions to the tensions experimentally observed and described in our phylo-analytic work, it is a satisfaction to feel that the early studies and formulations of my associates and myself have played some part in the development of broader envisagements in the fields of sociology and psychiatry.

TRIGANT BURROW

Editors' Note

All who knew Trigant Burrow, especially those privileged to be closely associated with him, were ever impressed by his zest for life, his thoughtfulness of every human being with whom he came in contact, and his deep conviction that man would come to recognize the need of a science of human behavior. His death on May 24, 1950, occurred while he was still at the height of his powers, with vital plans for future research and for the wider development of his thesis. It is a matter of poignant regret to the editors that he did not live to see the completion of this book.

Acknowledgments

The authors wish to express their deep appreciation of the assistance of Dr. William E. Galt in the preparation of Chapters VIII and IX.

The essays and sketches included in this volume are republished with the permission of the Mental Hygiene Society of Maryland.

Grateful acknowledgment is made for permission to quote from published works—

To The Beacon Press (Boston) for Trigant Burrow's "Prescription for Peace: The Biological Basis of Man's Ideological Conflicts," in *Explorations in Altruistic Love and Behavior*, edited by Pitirim A. Sorokin (1950);

To Harcourt, Brace and Company, Inc., for Trigant Burrow's *The Neurosis of Man—An Introduction to a Science of Human Behavior* (1949) and for his *The Social Basis of Consciousness—A Study in Organic Psychology* (1927);

To Alfred A. Knopf, Inc., for P. Kropotkin's *Mutual Aid—A Factor of Evolution* (1920);

To The Lifwynn Foundation (Westport, Connecticut) for Trigant Burrow's *The Biology of Human Conflict—An Anatomy of Behavior, Individual and Social* (The Macmillan Company, Inc., 1937);

To the McGraw-Hill Book Company, Inc., for Clyde Kluckhohn's *Mirror for Man—The Relation of Anthropology to Modern Life* (1949);

To the Orthological Institute (London) for Trigant Burrow's *The Structure of Insanity—A Study in Phylopathology* ("Psyche Miniatures"; London: Kegan Paul, Trench, Trubner & Company, Ltd., 1932) and for his "The Heroic Rôle —An Historical Retrospect," from *Psyche*, Vol. VI (1926); and

To The University of Chicago Press for W. C. Allee's *Animal Aggregations: A Study in General Sociology* (1931).

C. B. T.

A. P. S.

Contents

Introduction

The publication of Dr. Trigant Burrow's report of his thirty years' group investigations in human behavior* kindled my desire to republish the essays and stories collected in this small volume. For these vignettes were an early by-product of Dr. Burrow's highly significant experiment in group analysis. Along with others of Dr. Burrow's associates and students, it was my privilege to participate in this experiment. In prefacing this collection of essays and stories, I should, therefore, like to comment upon this basic group endeavor, and thus indicate the background from which these writings arose. A word in regard to this early integrative process in the field of man's relation to man seems especially appropriate in the midst of today's rapidly changing conditions and their growing demands for a wider, closer coordination of community thought and action.

In 1923, while serving as medical director of the Mental Hygiene Society of Maryland, I became interested in publishing a monthly journal, if only a leaflet, which I hoped would be of practical psychiatric value to the community. I outlined my idea to the president of the Society, the late Dr. Edward N. Brush, who will long be remembered for his wide interests and perspectives. Dr. Brush was heartily in sympathy with the plan and permitted me a free hand in selecting the material and directing the aims of the publication.

---

* Trigant Burrow: *The Neurosis of Man—An Introduction to a Science of Human Behavior* (London: Routledge and Kegan Paul, Ltd., and New York: Harcourt, Brace & Co., Inc., 1949).

It so happened that during this same period I was much absorbed in the studies in human behavior being conducted by Dr. Burrow. At that time Dr. Burrow was well along with the development of his pioneer community-investigations in accordance with his thesis that the neurosis of the individual inevitably implicates society at large. From 1911 his writings on psychoanalysis had consistently voiced his interest in this broader outlook. They made plain that "social custom is a derivative, not an elemental factor" in man's adaptation, and that the standard of conduct "we designate as 'normality' is nothing else than an expression of the neurosis of the race." However unrecognized, however anonymous, the elements or individuals composing human society were, in Dr. Burrow's view, definitely neurotic. Even as early as 1918 his intensive studies with his associate, Mr. Clarence Shields, were already setting the stage for the development of the technique in social readjustment he later called group analysis.

Although Dr. Burrow's social extension of his psycho-analytic studies seemed to the detached psychiatric onlooker of those days too sweeping and audacious, group analysis represented a natural and consistent evolution from years of interest, study, and research in interindividual behavior. The social groups constituted his laboratory setup, and the originality of his research lay in the opportunity it offered for the practical, everyday study of man's habitual interrelationships. Out of Dr. Burrow's intensive studies came the clear demonstration that neurotic disorders are not isolated and individual but that they are "essentially social in structure." He was speaking quite literally when he said, "We are all neurotics anonymous—'alcoholics anonymous' is but a subgrouping under this more encompassing social classification."

As I was deeply interested in Dr. Burrow's approach, I felt how fortunate it would be if I might secure his cooperation in launching the periodical I had in mind. I expressed to him this hope, and in the weeks that followed we devoted some time to threshing out the possibilities for such an avenue of community education. It developed that Dr. Burrow had himself been considering the need for just such a project, both as a sociological experiment and as a means of acquainting the larger community with the social nature of the neurosis. He felt that, while a periodical dealing with disturbed behavior-reactions would be of great value to the community, the undertaking would be a still more significant experiment if the material for publicaton were contributed for the most part by individuals who had themselves been subject to disturbed behavior-trends, and who had had the opportunity to orient themselves through a social analysis with respect to their own neurosis.

The upshot of our discussions was that Dr. Burrow very generously consented to collaborate in my publication in so far as his time would permit, and offered me the welcome opportunity of making this venture the medium of his contemplated project. In furtherance of this idea, Dr. Burrow made what appeared to me at the time the rather startling proposal that we enroll as members of our contributing editorial board those of his psychoanalytic patients who were already far enough along in the study of their own neurotic reactions to qualify for group analysis. However, he made it a condition that his name and those of his amateur collaborators would not appear in connection with my literary venture. As far as he, his associates, and his students were concerned, the undertaking was to be strictly anonymous.

My first reaction to Dr. Burrow's suggestion bespoke, I fear, a greater deference to my own cherished habituations and prerogatives than an appreciation of the forward-looking possibilities of his original idea. In response to long-standing, if unconscious, tradition it would appear to be our automatic tendency as psychiatrists to demand that a patient be kept in his place. In taking this position the psychiatrist is, of course, by no means unique. Everyone likes to be respected as the gracious dispenser of thoughtful beneficence, and our psychiatric loftiness is only another evidence of parental and didactic habits existing on every hand. And so I must confess that as a psychiatrist I felt no little trepidation concerning this uncanonical sponsorship of my literary enterprise. Nevertheless, as our plans took shape I could not help feeling that if this rather daring project could be made workable—if it were possible to organize an efficient body of workers consisting of patients who were undergoing group analysis because of the recognition of impediments in their own adaptation to the demands of everyday life—such an enterprise would undoubtedly yield results which would have a deep and intimate value for those of the community who were searching for guides to mental health, both in its individual and social phases.

A few days later Dr. Burrow, at my request, called a meeting of his students and the proposal was presented to them. From the outset they were keenly interested in participating in the group adventure. The plan was talked over at some length, and a few months later it was put into effect. This early development carried a historical significance which at the time I did not appreciate or even suspect. In relation to Dr. Burrow's investigations, it was the first social or group project undertaken by the initial phyloanalytic group in Baltimore. As regards the larger community implications of our endeavor, it marked the first time that a group of lay individuals who had studied behavior imbalances within themselves in an inclusive, social setting had attempted to impart the insights thus gained to a lay audience interested in the problem of mental hygiene.

The contributors to our cooperative enterprise numbered about seventeen. Included on the editorial staff, which acted in an advisory capacity and also contributed articles, were Dr. Burrow, his associate Mr. Clarence Shields, and myself. The students were individuals of average intelligence who, for the most part, had received more than the usual educational and cultural advantages; but none of them had displayed exceptional ability or had been distinguished for outstanding achievements in any field. Moreover, none had previously contributed essays or stories to current magazines; and, owing to their neuroses, they had not distinguished themselves by proficient participation in any systematic form of work. While it was our plan that all communications would be unsigned, the patients, or rather students, were to occupy a position of equal responsibility with us in the writing and selection of articles, as well as in the editorial criticism and revision of them. There was to be no allotment of subjects, the material contributed being entirely a matter of individual choice and initiative. We decided to name the journal *Mental Health*. Dr. Brush was more than pleased that the Mental Hygiene Society was to have this material for its periodical, and he was good enough to read and give his endorsement to each article as it was submitted for publication.

The plan proved most successful for the participants, as well as from the point of view of the community's interest and response. Writing and working together as members of the editorial board of *Mental Health* helped to bring about a marked sense of social responsibility in the students. As evidence of this, for the most part they later went on to positions of significance in civic, educational, scientific, and literary fields. The bulletin was warmly received by many readers, among them no less an authority than the late Dr. Stewart Paton, who on one occasion wrote me: "Congratulations on the excellent comment published in the latest number of Mental Health, June 1925. May I suggest that you make 'In Vain' just a little more popular in style, without changing the sense of what has been said, add a few practical illustrations and then give the paper a wide circulation." The essay referred to (p. 183) was an exposé of the futility and hypocrisy of legislation that allegedly aimed at the control of alcoholism but that in fact sorely beset the entire country and was responsible for much surreptitious, bootleg drinking on the part of young people, not to mention the mushroom growth of racketeering and crime, and the arbitrary restriction of the many by a fanatical few. Such a reaction from a scientist of the broad social perspectives of Stewart Paton was, of course, to be expected. At that time, Paton was among the few fearless pioneers in the field of human behavior. There was heartening commendation from so eminent a man of letters as Christopher Morley, and also from Floyd Allport, and from such journals as The Survey and Social Forces.

But at the same time there were those who found the forthright democratic policy of Mental Health unwelcome to their cherished mental and social habituations. Its radical departure from established precedent set us more and more at odds with prevailing psychiatric viewpoints and, consonant with the traditional epic of the minority, our salutary project was eventually compelled to discontinue. The three-year experiment, however, had left its mark upon the community and upon ourselves. It had consistently brought to a community audience the first intimations of a broad, biological conception of nervous and mental diseases. It had provided the student-contributors with the opportunity for an actual, working contact with an actual, working world, giving dynamic social expression to an important constructive principle in behavior therapy. According to this principle, the inhibited, maladjusted individual, when freed from social preconceptions and repressions, automatically reveals himself to be a personality endowed with initiative, interest, and capacity. Thus, our cooperative endeavor proved an entering wedge in the direction of social integration, of healthy community thinking and feeling.

In the stress of present-day circumstances, with the threat of another world war hanging over us all, the immediate moment offers an especially critical test for the emotionally insecure personality, and makes pertinent the republication of material bearing upon one of the earliest phases of Dr. Burrow's researches in community coordination. While certain types of neurotic personality will undoubtedly succumb to the increasing social and economic strain, it is equally true that other types will as surely come into their own by virtue of the very crisis with which the world is currently faced.

As we know, many distinguished and often creative personalities in the world—and the list includes such outstanding figures as Caesar, Leonardo da Vinci, Napoleon, Dostoevski, Elizabeth Barrett Browning, Chopin, Strindberg, and Tschaikovsky—are, in the light of recent knowledge, regarded as neurotics. But what are "neurotics"? As Dr. Burrow has said, "The neurosis is not restricted to a few peculiar, isolated individuals. The neurosis is social. It is a dislocation in behavior-pattern in which we all share in greater or less degree." Why, then, should we not expect to see competent social achievement in neurotic individuals as well as in the mythically styled "normal" personality? Indeed, is there not reason to expect that the repressed, sensitive type of individual harbors greater dynamic capacities than the everyday, go-as-you-please citizen among us? It is important to realize that neurotics are not wanting in either native ability or in balanced, intelligent motivation. They are individuals who, through the accidental combination of untoward environmental circumstances, have been so conditioned that they have lost the interest and the facility to gear into the current social and economic trend of things. They have both the words and the music, so to speak, but the words and the music are not yet harmonized into a common creative theme.

Psychiatry rightfully includes within its province the type of personality who somehow cannot make the grade, who perhaps has never made the grade. But it must not be overlooked that those who do "make the grade" and attain the "normal" criterion are also not lacking in neurotic behavior-trends. In their self-centered, competitive behavior they are often no less futile and obsessive than the clinical patient with his typically compulsive, unconscious reactions. The only difference is that, prior to Dr. Burrow's comprehensive group analysis of prevailing community-reactions, the behavior of the "go-getting" normal, with his driving competitiveness and "success," had never been subjected to intensive medical study and research. We have to admit that as a professional group we psychiatrists have been completely blind to the fact that success may be as unhealthy as failure; that those who make the grade may be, and in fact commonly are, as disturbed emotionally as those who fail to toe the mark arbitrarily imposed by the popular standards of "normality." Too generally the mark of success is the ability to run with the crowd, to keep abreast of the Joneses. We are still quite oblivious of the obsessive quality—the driving personalism and competitiveness—that now attaches to the attainment of society's eminently coveted goals. And it is not difficult to see why. As we psychiatrists, too, are "normal" and "successful," to attack the social phase of man's neurosis is to attack our own brand of social competitiveness and misadaptation.

If Dr. Burrow is correct in his thesis that the illness of the neurotic, however inept and mistaken a reaction, is a protest against the artificial standards of behavior espoused by the community, one would expect to find in this wider community-reaction the same mistakenness and ineptitude. If basically the community's reactions are also unsound, one would expect to find evidence of a common ground of deviation, of an unmistakable disorientation of interest and motivation in normal and neurotic alike. As a matter of fact, Dr. Burrow's group- or phylo-analytic investigations disclose the existence of just such a behavior parallel. They show that an ineptness of behavior exists no less in the wider community than in the neurotic personality, and that this ineptness colors and distorts the thinking and feeling of our government officials, of our administrative heads, of ministers, physicians, lawyers, educators, business executives, and, last but not least, of the specialists in behavior—psychiatrists themselves. In other words, society itself is neurotic; social man is himself in need of study and re-evaluation. In support of this position, Dr. Burrow's more recent investigations indicate that behavior imbalances, whether expressed in the reactions of the "normal" or the "neurotic," are traceable to conflict within the organism's internal tensional patterns and that this physiological disturbance is common throughout our so-called civilized life. There is no longer ground for any group of individuals to maintain that they must be anonymous—alcoholics or neurotics. All of us—individuals and nations—have a *common neurosis*. Man is neurotic.

The truth is, the individual we set apart as neurotic is really up against it. He occupies a position that is socially artificial, anomalous. He is penalized for a reaction that has been socially induced in him by the larger pattern of community behavior. The individual, whether isolationist or conformist, whether "neurotic" or "normal," has been conditioned in his reactions by his environment. If the community environment is deviate and ill, inevitably the individual is deviate and ill also. For the reactions of the neurotic are the direct issue of our so-called normal society. It is society that molds the social behavior of the individual. So that the adaptive incapacities of these personalities are necessarily an expression, however disfigured, of the adaptive level represented in "normal" community behavior. From the background of phylobiology, from the common basis of Burrovian patterns of tension, to single out a person as neurotic is artificial, unbiological. It is to deny him continuity with others. It is to deprive him, and ourselves as well, of a rightful sense of social solidarity—a condition essential to community balance and health.

It would seem, then, that the fundamental need of our times is not the treatment of the "neurotic" personality. What is needed is that social communities recognize the disordered nature of man's feeling; that they come to grips with the separative, personalistic mood now dominating "normal" interrelational behavior. What steps are we psychiatrists taking to prepare ourselves for this new orientation freshly opened to us? Does the direction of our training and equipment fit us for a clear envisioning and assessment of the problems that must confront us in the all-important field of social behavior? We cannot blink the increasing signs of man's growing need for coordination of purpose wherever groups—whether city-planning committee, labor-management meeting, Congress, or the councils of the United Nations itself—are called upon for decisive action.

There cannot be coordination, there cannot be unity and

cooperation, within social units if beneath the veneer of outer amenities there lurk the unconscious mechanisms of introversion, neuroticism, and conflict.

Contributing largely to this condition is the mechanism of emotional projection whereby a behavior-trend internal to oneself is denied acceptance and is attributed, instead, to someone else. The psychiatrist sees this mechanism operating constantly in his clinical work. But the mechanism of emotional projection is not restricted to the few or to the frail. It is a universal characteristic of the mind of man on our present level of adaptation. This mechanism is the factor that underlies and is answerable for our manifold expressions of affect— our various expressions of prejudice and of social bias. It is at the root of all our personal conflicts and social intolerances. Psychiatry must somehow come to recognize that this unconscious mechanism of projection, which the clinician now sees only in the mental patient, operates no less in the so-called normal processes of the clinician himself. This social insight undoubtedly entails a wrench for the conventional psychiatrist. As a psychiatrist myself, I well know how much of a wrench. But it is only through these broader social perspectives that psychiatry will attain adequate competence as an instrument of social welfare. It is only from such an inclusive basis that there will be the possibility of applying scientific method to legislative debate and governmental process. The value that such a method would have in the conduct of peace conferences in contrast to the emotional and, at times, violent recourses to insult and incrimination we witness in these current political gatherings hardly requires comment.

I should like to emphasize again that the sketches incorporated in this volume represent but an incidental aspect of Dr. Burrow's early researches in behavior analysis. They preceded by many years his discovery of a defect in the neural function of man's brain as a social organ—the defect to which he traced the systematization of affects and prejudices he later called the "I"-persona. There had not been at this time his demarcation of the affecto-symbolic segment or "third brain" with its evidence of reflex projection and a resultant reversal of human feeling and motivation. Group analysis was as yet little more than an experimental setup for the free observation of these reflex social mechanisms—the momentary attractions and repulsions of this "you" toward that "me," his fleeting loves and hates, his transient irritations and his equally evanescent infatuations. Such "normal" affects had not yet been brought to definite, objective observation, nor had the dominant role of the neuromuscular patterns of tension underlying these social reactions been definitely determined. All this was a later development—a development which the editors have tried to indicate in their comments accompanying the essays and stories.

It is hoped that the material gathered together in these pages may contribute its bit toward a freer, more democratic view of human behavior and its disorders. Whatever their shortcoming, these sketches do not stem from habitual conceptions or from "armchair" theorizing. They are the outcome of an original experiment in social behavior that gave opportunity for an objective group-survey of habitual, subjective group-reactions—an opportunity which, in view of our rapid social regroupings in pursuit of newer economic and industrial ends, needs extended community-application. In these amateur bits of writing that deal with common, everyday instances of "normal" behavior-distortions as these were participated in by the authors there are depicted emotional episodes in which each of us may readily see his own reflection.

When we have mustered sufficient social fortitude to recognize that we prefer to look at other people's defects of behavior rather than at our own—a pastime that occupies many people throughout most of the day—we shall discover in our various affect-reactions that what we most like to look at and criticize in others is invariably what we least like to look at and criticize in ourselves. This is but one of the numberless small items in the individual's behavior, the communitywide ramifications of which are presented for scrutiny in these brief essays reprinted now in collected form. The editors have made no attempt to revise the sketches. Their task has been merely to organize the essays and stories, and to prepare a framework for their presentation. I earnestly hope that these brief studies from *Mental Health*, written, as they were, in the very combat zone of man's inner conflict, may indicate the presence in the community of unrecognized emotional reflexes, and furnish constructive suggestions for a clearer orientation among us all.

Let me take this occasion to express a word of sincere acknowledgment to the readers of *Mental Health*, whose interest and appreciation kept our unique literary venture alive in spite of adverse pressure from psychiatric "standpatters." I am also grateful to the late Dr. Edward N. Brush, who wholeheartedly endorsed and supported the journal throughout its three years of publication. But, above all, I wish to reaffirm my indebtedness to Dr. Burrow and his students— an acknowledgment I made some twenty-odd years ago upon the discontinuance of our journal. I would like again to express my deep appreciation of the cooperation which Dr. Burrow and his group of anonymous contributors brought to this endeavor. Only his fundamentally altered envisagement of neurosis as a societal disorder—a concept which Dr. Burrow has consistently stressed—made this assistance possible.

Through his fearlessly aligning himself with students and patients in a common effort to put before the social community the common need for an adjustment usually thought to be restricted to the "neurotic patient," a thoroughly original and creative trend was introduced into the field of psychiatric research.

CHARLES B. THOMPSON

OUR COMMON NEUROSIS

CHAPTER I

Need of a Science of Human Behavior

Today, life is insecure and discordant the world over. Everywhere the species man is divided into quarreling groups. Although we cling to the hope that sometime, somehow, peace will come, the hope grows ever fainter as each day brings fresh evidence of a persistent impulse to disunity among human beings. The malignant shapes of destruction that haunt our thoughts are no mere figments of the imagination. They are real threats to our very lives, and they can materialize next month, next week, tomorrow.

A paradoxical feature of this dark picture is man's manifest desire to achieve peace. Never in all history has there been such a concerted effort toward this end. But even the most earnest endeavor seems destined to defeat, for the emotions of man do not support, with a steady and dedicated fervor, any effort toward harmony. Always there comes the moment when a deadly antagonism between individuals and between groups raises its head and proves itself stronger than the urge to cooperation and unity. What is the reason for this obdurate ambivalence in man's behavior? There is a challenge here to his inquiring mind—a challenge that, strangely enough, he has

never met. Though he is a gregarious animal, though the
processes that underlie his interrelational life are sociobiological, he does not study and observe his relation to his kind.
Obviously what is needed is an *objective*, a scientific investigation of the *subjective* processes that determine his behavior.

This small book is a by-product of just such an objective
research in the subjective field of human behavior. As such,
it reflects a developmental aspect of Dr. Trigant Burrow's
group or phylobiological* approach to the problem of conflict among men. In this approach, the light of science is
turned upon man's interrelational behavior with the purpose
of discovering the social and biological processes underlying
his conflicts and antagonisms. The first seven chapters
present the various symptoms of the divisive and artificial
motivation of human beings as observed and analyzed in the
earlier years of the group study. The eighth and ninth chapters
touch on the positive, dynamic aspects of phylobiology based
on the physiological discoveries made subsequent to the
period to which this book is largely devoted.

The course of phylobiology, like that of any other pioneer
investigation, was bound to meet with obstacles. Setting out
in an unknown realm, it necessarily was confronted by indifference or outright hostility born of man's confirmed
habituations. It was forced to devise new instruments and
new methods of observation. But to the inquiring mind,
such difficulties are only spurs to fresh effort toward the
solution of the problem under consideration.

Some thirty years ago, Dr. Burrow's formulation of the
two questions, "What is the matter with normality?" and "Is
there a norm of healthy interrelational behavior?" was the
starting-point of the scientific investigation of which this book

---

* The word "phylobiology," coined by Dr. Burrow, is a combination of
"phylon" (Greek for species) and "biology."

is a secondary result. In his foreword, he has related the circumstances that led to the formation of the phyloanalytic group. He has indicated the unique character of his group procedure, which has throughout the years been limited in its scope to purposes of research. Unique also was the relationship between the psychiatrists and the psychologists on the one hand, and the lay members of the group on the other. The accepted psychiatric procedure in which the doctor stands apart from the patient or student was no longer maintained. Instead, the reactions of *both* demonstrators and students were considered as material for objective observation and analysis. In this way a social method was introduced for the investigation of social behavior. Included in the group were neurotics and so-called normal people, representing different professional and economic aspects of society. The undertaking was no less human than scientific. It was the analysis of man in his living day. The members of the group worked together; and later on, as part of his experiment, Dr. Burrow reproduced the external conditions of the family dining-table which, in our culture, is the first social group or community encountered by each individual. In addition to the formal group sessions, the students concerned themselves with common projects, one of which was the preparation of the monthly paper, *Mental Health*, in which were published the stories and essays forming the nucleus of this book.

In their daily group analysis the students became more aware of the common motivation underlying their interrelational reactions—a motivation which up to that time each had thought belonged to himself alone. This experience gave impetus to their observation of social reactions everywhere. The material contributed to *Mental Health* reflected their awakening to their own disordered behavior and to a like disorder in the larger world beyond the laboratory group.

These vignettes and the accompanying comments not only furnish historical orientation with regard to phylobiology, but they also throw light on the type of material studied in the early days of group analysis.

The following essay, contributed by one of the group at that time, represents the point of view from which these pieces were written.

THE STARTING POINT

Man has been thinking for many thousands of years. To think has been his distinction. In his passage from the unknown to the known, it was ever man's thought that opened the way. With his thought man has developed philosophies, sciences, religions; fashioned laws and built up nations. He has discovered the years before man was and has projected his calculations to include the heavens. Through all the years he has pressed forward eagerly until today the products of his thought cover the earth with endless devices for his comfort and cultural advancement. It would seem there were no limit to the possibilities of man's thought.

And yet, though he has made phenomenal strides in his thinking, there is something amiss with the thought of man. Though man's thought has never ceased to progress in all matters that pertain to his physical environment, there are occasions in his emotional life when man is face to face with the demand for further thought and he ceases suddenly to think. Though there has been no problem too difficult, no uncertainty too forbidding, no "darkest Africa" too terrifying, he suddenly balks in the face of the jungle of his own emotional life. His interest, eagerness and love for adventure desert him. Where ordinarily his thought would function, now he suddenly

sinks back. Or he flashes up momentarily in fiery self-
defense only to retreat into impotent uncertainty, meekly
crying that what was good enough for his forbears is
good enough for him. Before the unknown reaches
of his own immediate emotional entanglements man
stops and, staring wildly, raises his hand in protest—"You
go too far," he exclaims. "It is enough. One must adhere
to family customs. I prefer the delusions of my fore-
fathers. War has its place. And the deceptions of peace
are soothing. This good old world of love and hate is
good enough for me." And so just where he would begin
to think, he stops. At the contemplation of his own life
he is baffled. At the starting point he complains and
defends. All thought vanishes. There is only self-interest
and self-indulgence.

It is not a new situation. Thought has ever been
tinctured with an emotional bias. But within the physical
sciences this bias has not retarded the onward progress
of man's thought. What is new to man is the growing
realization that his emotional life is a region that is
foreign to him—a region full of fear, superstition, personal interests and old habituations. And with it there
slowly comes the intimation that, in the face of this undiscovered wilderness of his own emotions, his thinking is
not thinking after all but rather the evasion of thought.

Proud of his achievements on land and sea, man becomes a frightened victim of delusion in the face of these
—his own emotional entanglements. Man, who has
harnessed the earth and conquered the air, who has in-
tuitively discovered the invisible forces of nature and her
universal laws, trembles and makes excuses in the face
of his own feelings and associations. At the starting point
of thought he cries out petulantly: "No, you are wrong.

The world is not round. The universe is not infinite. The world is flat. The world of my immediate horizon is the only world that exists. This flat world on which *I* look—this world of me here and you there, of secret family dissension and international intrigue, this flat scorched plain of my gains and your losses, this flat world that is mine—my home, my money, my aches, my pains and pleasures, my depressions and elations, my failures and successes—this is the world I like because this is the world that is mine." And so where thought might begin, man, who is lord over all, backs off into the secrecy of his closet and hugs his fanciful possessions to the delusion of himself.

No, it is not the fact of man's emotion that is new. What is new to man is the faint glimmering recognition that the emotion he calls his own is not his own, that he has appropriated it to himself for the satisfaction of himself. As man's thought has converted the crude materials of the soil into the delicate engines of industry, putting their uses to the economic service of mankind, his interest must now turn to man himself, and from the starting point of his own emotions he must shape these cruder products of his developmental heritage into the finer fabric of his thought.

Throughout the early years of the phylobiological research, the students examined as objectively as possible the social milieu in which we live. In an effort to arrive at the springs of disordered behavior, both individual and social, their attention was directed to aspects of our normal life that are accepted as commonplace, even trivial—for example, the ceaseless desire for superficial diversions or the lack of rapport in family life. Such habitual tendencies became subjects for thoughtful observation, as the following two pieces indicate.

ESCAPE

The greater part of our amusements and much of all of our living seems to be grounded in an effort to escape. We go to the theatre to escape boredom; we seek other people in order to get away from ourselves or we demand privacy that we may get away from others. From early childhood on we make an effort to escape from ourselves to something outside ourselves; to be concerned with our education, our work, our play, our families and our friends, not because of values we find in them but because they seem to offer an escape from some torment within ourselves. And each of these, in turn, leads us on inevitably to other interests. Each, though it does not satisfy, holds out the promise of something further on which will satisfy; each distracts us from an inquiry into the obsessive urge that drives us on. We are like the Iowa farmer who gets up early in the morning to plow corn to feed hogs to make money to buy land to get up earlier in the morning to plow more corn to feed more hogs to make more money to buy more land to get up earlier in the morning—! Pursuit becomes the thing and we are too busy with it to ask what it's all about. We need such a challenge as that to Jean Christophe by his uncle: "You want to make beautiful songs so as to be a great man and you want to be a great man, so as to make beautiful songs. You are like a dog chasing its own tail."

Perhaps if we were to question the nature of this ceaseless striving it might remind us of the senseless stampede of cattle. It seems hardly possible that such frenzied running after phantoms can satisfy our human needs. Perhaps, after all, there is nothing to escape from —nothing to escape to. Perhaps we can never get away from ourselves to others or from others into ourselves.

THE FAMILY AS A HANDICAP

If the neurotic invalid, during the period when he is trying to lift himself out of a serious depression, must necessarily remain within the home, he is definitely handicapped. The normal environment, within which he was accustomed to function naturally, now faces him as a standard at which he looks with terror as his ineffectual self moves about only with difficulty, if at all. But the general atmosphere of the home is not the only burden added to the inner conflict with which he has to struggle. There is the reaction of the individual members of the family. On the one hand they may sentimentalize over the invalid, showing their concern over his condition, thus substantiating his delusions. On the other hand they may grow very impatient with him because of his inability to throw off the fears that are so obviously unreal. Then there may be the grudge that the family has against him for time taken away from their own affairs, as well as for money spent on an illness that seems much more unreasonable than any infectious disease. Society, in the shape of friends, excuses only illnesses brought on by germs.

In any case the acute sensitiveness of the neurotic does not fail to register the pain any of these reactions may cause him. In his unbalanced state of mind there is needed very definitely an environment that is steady, an environment within which he will be accepted with neither criticism nor sentimentality, where he will be met with sympathy and, what is more important, with understanding. Here he can come face to face with his delusions and his fancies without fear or humiliation. When he can look at himself thus honestly he will realize that he is no worse than others, neither is he any better.

We laugh at the absurdities, we deplore the anguish of our so-called normal life, but we do not question our belief that it is unimpeachable; we do not doubt that normality is as solid as the ground we walk on. Science has not yet felt called upon to question the assumption that the present basis of man's interpersonal relations is sane and dependable. In the essay entitled "Who Are the Insane?" the writer expresses her feeling of the great need to challenge the generally accepted opinion that our "normal" behavior is a healthy expression.

WHO ARE THE INSANE?

It was the story of a casualty of the World War that suggested the question raised here. Sensitive, capable, highly educated, he sacrificed his life work and became a unit in the drill for bloodshed. But the things the training required him to do filled him with horror and he finally lost his reason.

His story is trite enough—it is only one of many. But we have not grasped its full significance if our interest ends with the placing of an insane man within the walls of an institution. The important point for our consideration is that it is we—all of us—who have placed him where he is. In our occasional brief moments of clear thinking we seem to sense vaguely the utter lack of reason that impels us to destroy life by way of settling our disputes. But that is the method we have always used, and we like to delude ourselves into thinking that what has received the stamp of social approval must be right.

It is this delusion concerning the force of social approval that has caught us all in its subtle grip. It makes us afraid to dress, think, act differently from our neighbors. It makes each of us want to be better, richer, more brilliant than anyone else. It is responsible for our social competition, our industrial exploitation, finally our warfare. Being in its grip, we inevitably struggle against an understanding of our delusion. But in so far as there is a dissatisfaction with the present state of things, there is the need to see clearly the tendencies within ourselves that are responsible for it. A knowledge of these tendencies is not a matter of academic learning. There is required merely an understanding of the daily contacts among ordinary human beings, among ourselves. With this understanding we shall soon sense the fallacy of the conviction with which each of us claims his family to be the finest, his religion the truest, his country the greatest. It is such fallacies as these that goad us on to personal enmities, social feuds, international wars. If we are earnest in our purpose to weigh these things in the balance, we must be prepared to face the disquieting conclusion that there is insanity even among those of us who would not be technically regarded as "insane."

It is easier to go along with the crowd than it is to make the effort to examine the springs of its action. It is so much less trouble to accept the popular fallacies that mark our social interchange than to examine them with the objective attitude of the scientist. This marked inertia of man in his approach to interrelational problems was noted in the early years of group analysis, and forms the material of the following essay.

EASY SOLUTIONS

Under the protection of the social consensus the human mind is prone to methods of reasoning that demand the least expenditure of thought. Inference is so much easier than examination. Its demand upon our energies is so much less. "It looks like" or "it seems as if" are far handier recourses for disposing of the facts of life than "it may be shown to be" or "it is." The truth is that of all our organs the brain is the laziest. From habits of long contamination with false impressions it tends to balk in its function and, wherever it can, it finds a way to avoid its appointed work. "Nice discriminations are troublesome," remarks George Eliot. "It is so much easier to say that a thing is black, than to discriminate the particular shade of brown, blue or green to which it really belongs. It is so much easier to make up your mind that your neighbor is good-for-nothing, than to enter into all the circumstances that would oblige you to modify that opinion."

This prevalent mental tendency is explicable only on the ground that there exists in the social mind today much the same tendency to false and easy inference that characterizes the mind of the single individual. It must not be supposed, however, that this lax manner of reasoning is by any means confined to the uneducated or even to people of average education. Instances of these quite easy short cuts are characteristic of many types of mind that are supposedly trained and scientific. Typical of such lapses even in the scientific mind is the tendency of the sociologist who, wishing, for example, to correct conditions as he finds them, attempts to organize a different regime without having first analyzed the deeper causes responsible for the disorders present in the social order as it now exists. The medical mind is likewise answerable for many current views that rest upon no sounder foundation than that of offhand, casual inference. Consider this familiar bit of sophistry frequently expressed by the lay mind but sponsored in reality by the often too indolent methods of physicians themselves. It is admitted that there exists throughout the country a condition of social unrest, and coincident with this general situation there exists among various individuals an increase of nervous manifestations. But the mere concurrence of these two phenomena, social restlessness and individual restlessness, has been sufficient to warrant the conclusion that the latter condition is necessarily the result of the former. It is not thought necessary to penetrate to the deeper strata of causation and seek to discover whether there may not exist beneath the surface a factor that is common to both and that is equally responsible for this common condition. Or let us cite another fallacy likewise substantiated in presumably scientific quarters. If a patient shows simultaneously a loss of weight and a loss of interest—or "nervousness"—it is so easy to regard the two circumstances as correlated in such a manner that the loss of weight is assigned as the cause of the lack of interest. This is in line with the popular fallacy which assumes that nervous disorders are invariably to be traced to physical disability. In point of fact there are very many nervous individuals who are not underweight at all, who are indeed quite stout, just as there are very many persons who are underweight and who are not nervous at all, but are in fact quite "normal." Yet despite this obvious discrepancy in logical process, this quite accidental concurrence between an individual's mental condition and his physical condition has been credited with the validity of an organic sequence.

Of course this is the easy solution. This is the solution that does not demand an expenditure of energy in the earnest concentration requisite to scientific analysis and comprehension. But it is of great significance for us that this tendency to the adoption of the easy solution in all circumstances is a frailty that characterizes the social mind not less than the individual. We should recognize to what extent physicians and sociologists themselves hold the unthinking attitude of the layman toward these problems. We should recognize that in their unfamiliarity with the essential factors in question, professional men too often disseminate opinions which are uttered for purposes of mere social edification and which, in their hastiness and superficiality of view, do not begin to approach the underlying causes of the conditions supposedly under examination.

There may be some who will say, "But what about the science of psychology? What about psychiatry and psychoanalysis? Do not these disciplines investigate normal and abnormal behavior-processes?" Undoubtedly they do. Psychology has done invaluable work in the study of the individual and his various complex activities. It has investigated mental processes, analyzed their component parts, and discovered their relation to physical functions. Psychiatry has contributed much in uncovering the secret springs of disordered behavior in the individual patient, and in relating individual difficulties to certain environmental pressures. Freud and the psychoanalysts performed an incalculable service when they delved into the emotional conflicts of the individual neurotic, throwing a flood of light upon hitherto mysterious processes underlying disordered behavior. But none of these disciplines has investigated the processes underlying normality. They have not questioned the validity of normality as a criterion for evaluating human behavior. As a matter of fact, the therapeutic aim of psychiatry and psycho-analysis is to restore the patient to the ordinary normal life generally accepted as healthy. It seemed to the initiators of group- or phylo-analysis that an altered frame of reference was demanded. It seemed imperative to dispense with all pre-conceived ideas of normality and approach the problem of man's interrelational behavior through an investigation into the basic feeling and thinking of the race as an organic whole. The attitude toward the problem adopted by the participants in group analysis is exemplified in the next essay.

CRIME AND THE NEUROSIS

The dramatis personae of this little drama from real life are four, a man and his wife, a daughter of fourteen and a son of sixteen, two intelligent, modern and generally delightful young people. The playlet deals with a per-fectly commonplace situation. The parents are fairly well supplied with worldly goods, at least they support com-fortably an automobile which serves more or less as the villain of the plot. Running the machine themselves, the parents have made it their business to jitney the children to and from school and to show them the greatest possible consideration in the arrangement of the automobile schedule otherwise. The companions of the children come from families mostly wealthier than their own, and they have had little difficulty in providing for themselves substitute motor transportation whenever a congestion of family engagements has threatened them with the discomforts inseparable from trolley service. In the course of time the son secures his license as a driver of the family car and the daughter begins to have evening engagements in a somewhat different social set than that of her brother. With an increase in the demand of the young people the automobile service threatens to thin out, and there is consequently much grumbling on their part at the prospect of being deprived of that which they have automatically been accustomed to consider their inalienable rights. The crisis is reached in the reaction of the parents to the situation facing them, and Father's lines read: "I simply cannot understand these children. When I was a boy the street car was quite good enough for me." And Mother, taking the cue, replies: "Yes, you and I certainly did not feel this way when we were their age. Their extravagant ideas are altogether inexcusable."

In its outward aspect the situation is colorless enough to be of no interest whatever outside the walls of the inconspicuous household. But from another point of view it is of the most far-reaching significance, for there is involved in this seemingly trivial family situation a tendency that underlies practically everything we do. Here we have parents solemnly shaking their heads over the luxury-loving tendencies of the children they have themselves encouraged to love luxury, and failing entirely to realize their own involvement in the situation. But the family is merely a replica in miniature of the whole of society, and the relationship between parent and child is exactly identical with that which exists between society and the individual. Speaking broadly, this relationship is twofold and confused. The individual is what he is because society is what it is. But society is for some reason unwilling or unable to recognize this fact. We look at the individual and, failing to realize the involvement of all in that which each one is, we stand aside to praise the man whom we consider good and great, and want to punish him who seems to warrant our disapproval.

Take for example the attitude which society assumes toward the individual who happens to develop into a so-called criminal. There stands out conspicuously the repeated demand upon our criminal courts to mete out prompt and severe punishment in order to discourage crime. I do not approach the question as one who speaks with authority in the matter of the criminal law or of the criminal courts. I realize too fully the difficulty encountered in the practical application of a cold legal enactment to a situation throbbing with all the human emotion involved in the commitment of a crime. At the moment this particular phase of the crime problem, however perplexing, seems altogether negligible. What is of concern is the social implication that lies in our tendency to look to the criminal courts to bring about a lessening of crime. In making this demand upon the judges we unconsciously admit our belief that it is those alone who have committed a crime who are to be considered responsible for the commitment of crime.

We are as unwilling to realize our involvement in a situation of which we disapprove as were the parents of the luxury-loving children. We are like the parents in our tendency to blind ourselves to the part we play in the development of the criminal. We do not want to see that were we not as we are, the criminal would not be as he is. Such an attitude reflects our resistance to a sensing of our involvement, and is altogether incompatible with the social consciousness in which *Mental Health* is interested. Such a social consciousness would give the criminal, as it would give the neurotic, an opportunity to realize that the tendency within him which makes him seem abnormal has not developed spontaneously within himself as an individual.

Over and over again there has been stressed in these

columns the point that an individual neurosis is inconceivable aside from an environment of which it is the inevitable outcome. From this point of view the only approach to the victim of a nervous disorder that can be made with any conviction is through the development of a social environment that is itself not neurotic. And that which applies to the neurotic individual and his environment applies with equal force to the criminal and his environment. The tendency to crime is in no way different from the tendency to nervous disorders. It is inconceivable that individual nervous disorders will develop in a community that is itself in a socially healthy condition. It is equally inconceivable that such a community could foster a tendency to crime.

It would seem, then, that the time has come for an understanding of the destructive trends in man's "normal" adaptation throughout the race. We need to see that man's judgment is clouded, his observation distorted. In relation to himself his brain simply does not work with the clarity and precision that characterize its processes in relation to the physical world. And so we accept as inevitable such socially imbalanced expressions as prejudice, hyperexcitability, and capricious irritation, even though they bring war in their train. We are so completely inured to the condition that we do not see it as material for objective investigation.

One of the essays published in *Mental Health* more than twenty years ago urged the pressing need for recognition of this situation.

BLIND MAN'S BUFF

Dullness is an infirmity that is as obstinate as it is general. The reason is that by the very nature of the condition we are dependent in our quest for a remedy

upon the organ that is the seat of the disease. I refer to
no other organ than the brain itself. There is no question
but that, owing to its long contamination by unhealthy
impressions, the brain has become the most sluggish of
all the organs of the body. No other organ is so inert in
its function or tends so habitually to distort the processes
natural to it. And with our present limited equipment for
observation, the more we consider our dilemma the more
serious does the outlook become. For the situation bids
fair to continue unabated unless science, by taking
thought, can devise some process of technique whereby it
may furnish the brain of man with the necessary faculty
for enabling it to contemplate its own dull faculties—
particularly the faculty with which it has thus far attempted to deal with disorders of which the brain itself is
the particular seat.

With respect to any other of our functions our attitude
is entirely different. We readily note the frequency with
which other organs become impaired. Looking about us
and observing people with a defect of hearing, it is plain
to us that it is due to some impairment of the auditory
channel. We do not hesitate to admit how frequently
there occur defects of vision and we readily attribute them
to refractive errors or other disturbances in the function
of the eye. Abdominal pain, loss of appetite and weakness
are admittedly occasions prompting us to seek medical
aid because of the indication they give of some disturbance
of function within the organs of digestion. Thoughtful
people are very careful to avoid remaining any length of
time in close, ill-ventilated rooms because of the menace
of impure air to the lungs and respiratory tract. Even
the slightest and most superficial wound is immediately
safeguarded against deeper infection through the prompt

application of effective antiseptics. There is today a very wide-reaching tendency toward the careful selection of foods with reference to their chemical values in order that through a balanced diet the organism throughout may preserve a state of health. Among intelligent persons any sign of impairment of the processes of elimination is straightway regarded with suspicion, and an immediate investigation is sought with a view to disclosing the process or organ that is at fault.

With disorders of the brain the attitude of people everywhere is the exact reverse of this. Parallel disturbances within the function of the brain are actually neglected or even evaded. We sedulously protect from discovery and withhold from the needed remedy the many inadequacies besetting the function of the organ of reason. If our opinions show evidence of inadequacy through defect of logic, instead of seeking a remedy for them we rush to their defense. We amass all manner of specious "argument" under which to hide their inherent weakness. In a word, where there exists an impairment of function in any part or organ of the body outside of the brain we give ourselves over freely to medical skill, placing our confidence and our dependence upon the remedial measures it brings to our aid. But when the brain gives indication of deficiency of function as evidenced in habits of unwarranted prejudice, of opinions unsupported by facts, and of fantasies unrelated to reality, our sympathy and confidence lie wholly with the inadequacies of prejudice, fantasy and unreason, and we regard with suspicion and resentment whatever mediation may be offered to arrest such destructive brain reactions.

It is evident that there is the need for recognizing and facing squarely this serious impediment to scientific inquiry into the causes of mental disturbance depending solely upon our own individual impressions. As long as we are prone to protect our impressions from candid observation and analysis, a scientific attitude toward mental manifestations (disturbances of reason) is anteriorly precluded. Surely it is evident that a basis of observation that does not limit itself to that of the individual is the only recourse which will secure scientific perspective toward the individual's basis of impressions. Only such a development of methods as will enable the individual to stand apart in a spirit of objective scrutiny of his own processes will make it possible for the human mind to observe its own function and bring logical remedy to the illogical processes represented in the impaired functions within the organ of the brain.

The objective attitude outlined in the previous essay has never been applied to our so-called normal processes. The very word "normal" is a misnomer. It implies that in the field of interrelational behavior there has been established a norm of health such as obtains in other domains of medicine. But, as Dr. Burrow was the first to point out, there is no such behavioral norm. Every human culture has its own concept of what constitutes "right" behavior. Yet in every case this concept is a mental, ulterior evaluation of a mystical something designated as "the good." It has little or no relation to the fundamental balance of the organism in its response to the environment. Whether it is wholesome for the organism of man, whether from the biological point of view it constitutes a fitting response to the environment, are questions that have never been asked. Meanwhile the species is torn with strife, both individual and social. We are rapidly approaching the point where division among us is so violent that actual destruction of the race is frequently talked of as a possibility.

The student who wrote the following essay thinks of the problem as a physician thinks of an epidemic.

PUBLIC HYGIENE AND NERVES

In the consideration of contagious diseases it is becoming more and more a commonplace that the treatment of an individual patient is of relatively little importance. The vital point of attack is the source of supply of the germs responsible for the illness. Enlightened medical opinion has transferred its interest from the cough and temperature of a tubercular patient to the sanitarium in which he is to be segregated and to the sanitary condition of the home and factory to which he may some day return. With a knowledge of the connection between the water supply and typhoid fever, the burden of this problem to a large extent was handed over by the physician to the sanitary engineer. The wisdom of such procedure is now so well established that an entirely new field of medical practice is being developed. In this hopeful field the statistics that command our respect represent not the number of patients cured, but the number who never fall ill.

Much human suffering has been eliminated as a result of the efforts of physicians concerned with questions of public hygiene. And even greater progress can be foreseen in the discovery of germs and their methods of inoculation, and consequently in a prevention of the illness that might otherwise occur. By way of contrast this progress leaves in deep shadow the vast field of human suffering involved in nervous disorders. In the case of these sufferers there is no hope of segregating a germ and carrying it to the laboratory to place it under the microscope. The patient and his symptoms are one and inseparable, and the approach to him can be based on no precedent to be found in the realm of physical illness. Even with that approach established, often a far greater difficulty is involved in an attempt to include in a consideration of his condition the background from which it was developed. However, even in the case of nervous disorders there may be a field of inquiry that parallels roughly that of public hygiene in the case of physical disease. The most casual reading of almost any daily newspaper suggests situations responsible for mental confusion of every possible degree. A child runs away from home because he cannot keep up with his school work and is taunted by his fellow pupils. Inevitably the thought suggests itself that the trouble may lie primarily not in the child but in the school curriculum. A young telephone operator has to be placed in an institution where she is quite calm as long as she can take the initiative in speaking, but if some one speaks to her first she becomes violent. A sacrifice such as this can direct our attention upon our whole industrial system. A young man commits suicide while his fiancée is busy with her preparations for their coming marriage. Such an incident shocks us immediately out of our accustomed complacency. Once we begin to think, we shall find that it challenges the entire system of our social life.

To these dramatic instances there must be added the great army of apparently normal individuals who find themselves thwarted in their efforts to "carry on" in the everyday competitive world. These too demand attention along with the more acutely ill. There can, then, be no question as to the vastness of the problem suggested. There is, however, the very vital question as to whether we shall be satisfied with an attempt to cure the individual patient or whether we consider it our responsibility to trace his difficulty to its source and to deal with that. This responsibility is no light one. No method has as yet been advanced as to how it can be undertaken. In the schools of public hygiene there is to be found only the vaguest analogy in the way of a program. Here is a task for a pioneer and one with no small degree of courage. In any case it may be worth while to consider the possibility of an approach to the problem of nervous disorders which has as its main object their prevention rather than their cure.

Group analysis was an experiment and, as with all pioneer efforts in the field of science, errors were made and more than one false turning. Yet out of the preliminary spadework emerged the new science of human behavior—the thoroughly radical thesis of phylobiology.

CHAPTER II

Group Analysis

The bedrock of phylobiology is the thesis that the race of man is an organismic unit of which individual human beings are the elements. The seventeenth-century astronomers were aware of the force of gravity, yet they had little data on which to rest a solid body of interpretation. Similarly, in the first gropings of phylobiology toward an understanding of interrelational reactions, there was an intuitive perception of an integrating principle in human behavior. From the beginning there was dimly sensed the presence of a common, spontaneous motivation that binds the elements of the species into a biological group. From this point of view, disordered behavior on the part of an individual is merely a symptom of a vast societal disorder that has prevented the organism of man from reacting as a unitary whole. The concept of the species man as a societal organism was the basis for the inauguration of a study that was to be a group and not an individual analysis. The group was envisaged as an organismic unit, not as a collection of individuals such as a class in school or an audience in a lecture hall.

In the early years of the experiment, it is true, emphasis was placed upon the behavior of the individual. This emphasis was inevitable because every member of the group had been conditioned, in common with all human beings, to approach problems of behavior from his own personal viewpoint. As time went on, however, the neurosis came to be recognized more and more as a social phenomenon. Gradually the material under observation was identified as a commonly disordered, divisive mood, preoccupied at all times with images of self-advantage. This common mood, shared alike by neurotic and normal, hid itself under all sorts of disguises designed to conceal ulterior aims. Day after day, the motivation of the students was shown to be other than it appeared to be. Day after day, the demonstrators pointed unwearyingly to the need of recognizing the flaw in man's so-called normal behavior. They felt the necessity to see that the reactions of both individual and group were at all times dominated by affect, a term used in phylobiology to indicate wishful, self-biased feeling.

During that early phase of the group work, however, no technique had been developed through which the student could come to grips with his affect as a process internal to his organism. He could merely follow the traditional approach to pathological behavior, and observe and record symptoms. Many of the sketches that appear in this book were written with no aim other than that of presenting as clearly as possible the various aspects of normal life that impressed the writers as bizarre or disordered. Nevertheless, they may be of interest to students of man's behavior because they reveal the need of a basic approach to interrelational problems. The following piece is an example. The writer unconsciously expresses the habitual mood of man in approaching our ineptness of adaptation.

This is the title of a book which was handed to a lonely and disappointed woman by a lonely and unhappy man. These two people, both unusually endowed, should have been outstanding personalities, but through some fluke both have been conspicuously inhibited. This book by Clara E. Laughlin is not literature and cannot be taken seriously. It is all the more significant that these two people, both of whom have reached maturity, could be drawn under the spell of its title.

The fact is, everybody is lonesome. We find ourselves in the midst of relationships which, when tested, prove wholly inadequate to meet the need in each of us for companionship. Old people are lonely, married people are lonely, unmarried people are lonely; mothers of grown children are peculiarly lonely and little children sob themselves to sleep in an utter bewilderment of loneliness.

This loneliness of little children must give us pause. If the foundation of our agony is laid in the nursery, the early environment of the developing human being must be questioned.

One cannot think of a nursery that is not filled with utter confusion. Antagonisms seem to predominate. There is small wonder. Parents, having had standards of right and wrong, good and bad imposed upon them, reflect this inheritance in their efforts to solve their problems. Every mother meets her baby on the basis of her personal bias which she imbibed from her family, and every father punishes his son according to the idiosyncrasies he has developed out of his family history. Here is the subtle source of the favoritism that is so subtly reflected in the nursery that the tempestuous tantrums that occur seem to burst full grown from the tiny inmates. The result is a bad boy in tears with a good brother or sister looking on.

Out of the nursery of Adam and Eve, Cain slew his brother. "The Lord had respect unto Abel and unto his offering: But unto Cain and to his offering he had not respect." Abel was a good boy, Cain was a bad boy. The situation in which there was the good brother and the bad brother involved the deep-seated antagonism as in a vise-like grip, and murder was the only solution of the problem.

Aren't we still being nurtured in the atmosphere of Eve's nursery? Aren't we still being burdened by the good and bad which worked havoc on Cain and Abel? Aren't we still breeding the naïveté which fails to recognize that our menacing competitions, our international wars are merely the same issues, looming in larger aspect, that are met with in the nursery?

The nurseries of today are filled with children who are differentiated one from another, good children and bad children, stupid children and clever children, good-natured and ill-tempered children, one kind of children contrasted with the opposite kind of children. So each of us grows up looked upon as some special kind of person, looking at himself as opposed to some other person different from himself. We are either more attractive or less attractive than somebody else. An eternal comparison. Until we realize the destructive nature of this mental background of differentiation in which all our thinking arises we shall remain potential murderers. Surely this is not the fate encompassing us.

The organic life with which each of us comes into the

world is sufficient endowment to throw off this age-old habituation. And though the individual may be unable to free himself from the trap of isolation in which he finds himself, it is possible for us together to accept our brothers as like ourselves rather than look upon them as different, and thus to lift the curse of loneliness that was put upon those first two children.

This essay is written with earnestness. There is no question that the writer is speaking out of a deeply felt personal sense of isolation. She is a woman with a conspicuous capacity for devotion, to whom our so-called normal life of artificial get-togetherness is torture. Yet from the standpoint of later developments in phylobiology her comment, as all such comments, is lacking in perspective and objectivity. It is a rumination, and a rumination with a strong undercurrent of sentimentalism. The vague allusion at the end to a possible acceptance of our brothers as like ourselves is merely the voicing of an aspiration in regard to behavior. A bacteriologist, looking through his microscope at the bacterial agent of some infectious disease, does not bewail the fact that he belongs to a race exposed to such dangers. Nor does he voice aspirations in respect to the future. He applies himself completely to his material. He keeps on looking through his microscope and performing various experiments until he knows what he needs to know about those bacteria. But in regard to his own behavior man has had no recourse other than to take a wishful, sentimental attitude.

Ordinarily, writing a comment on the loneliness of man would seem to be a wholesome activity, but in the later group-sessions it was possible to bring into the open the affect underlying such apparently constructive expressions. These expressions were shown to be what they actually were—indulgence in self-biased emotion. For years the chief aim of the analysis was the challenge of such affect-reactions in individual and group. Invariably the students reacted to such challenge with a fiercely defensive response. No member of the group, whether leader or student, was exempt from the feeling that he must always be "right." But painful as was the process of such continual affect-frustration, it proved to be an essential preliminary to the later, more developed stages of the laboratory investigation. For it is man's affect, or his self-biased feeling, that has obstructed every effort he has made in the past to look objectively at his own behavior.

Affect, then, is not native feeling that springs spontaneously as the organismic response to an environmental stimulus. Biologically it is not genuine. It is concerned with the prestige of one's artificially isolated self. One of the important findings of phylobiology was the existence of a pseudopersonality in each individual. The following sketch indicates the faint sensing of a condition which afforded material for laboratory investigation during many years.

THE CALENDAR OF CONFORMITY

Solomon Grundy born on Monday
Christened on Tuesday
Married on Wednesday
Sick on Thursday
Worse on Friday
Died on Saturday
Buried on Sunday
This is the end of Solomon Grundy

This "Song of Solomon" is typical of our mental attitude toward our days. Waking with the thought "Oh! this is blue Monday, and I have to go back to my stupid

job" or "It's Christmas morning, the children will soon
be coming to see what Santa Claus has put in their
stockings," the day stands to us only as a peg on which
to hang those things which modern existence forces us to
crowd into our daily routine. And so great has this force
become, or rather so unlimited our yielding to it, that we
have lost sight almost entirely of the real significance of
the twenty-four hours that pass between the rising of the
sun on one morning and the next. We forget that the
days during which Mr. Grundy underwent that great
variety of experiences were significant, not because of
those experiences, but merely because they were days. Of
such vital importance seems to us the comparatively slight
difference in the character we have fastened on each day
of the week, that it is well-nigh impossible for us to
realize that fundamentally they are all just exactly alike.
Try it for yourself and see. Try to imagine yourself in a
situation in which it had not been decreed that on Sunday
those who want to, go to church, that on Monday children
return to school and adults to their places of business,
on Tuesday one group of people does a certain thing, on
Wednesday another group something else, and so on and
so on *ad infinitum*. Simple though the task may seem, it
carries with it the necessity of wiping out the whole
phantasmagoria of our everyday civilization. Far fetched
it may seem and useless, and without further thought, it
is so.

But that which has happened to give to each day
what, from this point of view, we may call a false personality can be traced through practically every avenue
of our daily activities. It is the driving force that makes
our stooping under the burden of social conventions of
vastly greater importance to us than the giving a free

rein to the vital forces within us so that we can really
live in the full meaning of that word. Most striking of all
is the fact that what we have done to our days we have
done to one another, and by reflection each unto himself
as well. Having fastened a false personality upon myself
and upon you, how can the real *I* enter into communication with the real *you*? The answer is self-evident, but we
continue to search in vain for it in clinics and sanatoria.
How long must this vain search last?

The question asked at the close of this vignette has been
asked in many different guises through the ages. One thinks
of Pirandello's plays, of Elsa confronted with the enigma of
her lover's identity, of Hamlet's cry, "You would pluck out
the heart of my mystery." Man has long recognized this condition, but he has only talked about it. It remained for the
twentieth century to ask, "What are the processes, social and
physiological, that lie behind man's pseudopersonality?"

Looking back from the solid ground of proven fact on
which phylobiology stands today, it is interesting to see in
the preceding essay a groping toward the essentials of the
problem. The essay presents an example of social habituation.
It deals with give-and-take affects between people in a community, and indicates that these affects are substituted for
what the author calls "vital force," but what in phylobiology
would now be called the primary feeling of the organism.
Broadly speaking, this was the point to which group analysis
had progressed at that time. The problem was envisaged as
social and interrelational, having to do with wishful feeling or
affect. But for many years to come, the patient gathering of
data and the daily observation of man's emotional reactions to
his image-ridden environment were to form the chief activity
of the laboratory.

CHAPTER III

Affect or Emotional Bias

Feeling is a most important aspect of man's life. It is primitive and organismic and serves a basic function in relating man to his fellows. In the previous chapter we suggested that all is not well with man's feeling, that it has become disordered throughout. It no longer relates us clearly and directly to others but has become restricted, prejudiced, self-centered. But what has occasioned this common disorder within the sphere of man's feeling? This is a question Dr. Burrow asked himself early in his group researches. The answer came only slowly, as a result of intensive application in a laboratory of human behavior. It is in essence a simple answer. But it requires a consideration of the process of attention and of man's symbol-forming function.

Basically, attention is the process through which organism and environment are related as a total, interfunctioning unit. This direct and closely coordinated interfunctioning between organism and environment is characteristic of the infant today, as it was characteristic of the phylogenetic infancy of the race. It is the matrix out of which more specialized responses emerge. Human beings never completely lose touch with this total, physiological relation to their environment. The great pleasure derived from feats of physical skill is due in large part to the close coordination between factors internal and external to the organism. The scientist, the tennis player, the carpenter are successful in proportion to their capacity to become one with the material they handle. Even in this very limited experience of integration with his surroundings, man becomes deeply content.

In our everyday life we do not usually think of attention as having such a broad, encompassing function. Most people are accustomed to regard it only in its intellectual, "schoolroom" aspect, as it relates us through words and symbols to the external world. But this mental aspect is merely part of the larger attentive process—a process that is essential to the balanced function of the organism as a whole. To quote Dr. Burrow:

> In saying that attention is the process that primarily relates the organism to the outer world, our definition of attention covers the most instinctual and elementary, as well as the most intellectually specialized or symbolically complex reactions of the organism. If we consider the simpler mode of attention as manifested in the animal, we find it to consist of a process that relates the whole organism physiologically to the whole environment. . . . Undifferentiated or whole attention, as it exists in the animal, and primarily of course in man, is essential to viability and survival. Through the organism's instinctual attention it secures food, finds shelter, adapts itself to changes in temperature, senses danger, seeks its mate; and in all its external relations the health and integrity of the organism is dependent upon the process of attention. (*The Neurosis of Man*, p. 70.)

As Dr. Burrow says, man has the native capacity for undifferentiated or whole attention. But in man there has developed also a specialization of the attentive process which is not shared by any other animal species. This specialization involves predominantly the cerebral cortex, the visual and auditory senses, together with the muscles and nerves of the tongue and larynx. Through the exercise of this specialized part-function, the organism of man is capable of relating itself to the environment through language and the employment of the symbol. This special function of the total organism selects parts or indices of an object or condition in the external world and reproduces vocally or otherwise a symbol that stands for the whole object or condition. For example, the word "lightning" is a sign or symbol for a tremendously complex natural phenomenon. Such signs or symbols are of course completely valid and satisfactory. Because of the generic commonness of our sense organs, we easily reach consensual agreement in respect to external objects and conditions. This consensual meaning of the symbol is the basis of that classification of phenomena and grasp of relational sequences which we call science. By means of his symbolic attention man has mapped the external universe. Were it not for the sign or symbol it would be impossible to deal effectively with many complex features of the physical world.

But in the sphere of man's feeling—the sphere that primarily relates him to his fellow human beings—an untoward complication has risen. His feeling no longer flows out in natural fullness to the objects and people surrounding him, but instead it has become blocked, restricted, and has turned back upon him. For man has attempted to negotiate his whole process of feeling through the projective part-function of the brain. He has made the mistake of applying the selective, symbolic mechanism to total sensations and feelings internal to the organism. He has abstracted and labeled these feelings as he has labeled trees and stars and skies. He tries to project and manipulate them as he manipulates his symbols of external objects. But this cannot be done with one's feeling-processes. Feeling is primary, total, organismic. True feeling can be experienced and expressed only by the organism as a whole. It is a reaction that is completely incapable of being mediated through sign and symbol. When feeling is channeled through the restrictive part-function of the symbolic segment it becomes disordered. It becomes partitive feeling or affect, and is divorced from the response of the organism as a whole. To quote Dr. Burrow in *The Structure of Insanity:*

> Internal feeling-states are not objective, not symbolizable. They are not to be perceived by the eyes or the projective senses, because they are not processes that occupy a place in front of the eyes or exteroceptors. Our attempt to project sensations that are essentially internal is due to our having inadvertently attempted to apply the partitive function of attention to processes which belong to the systemic or integral system of attention expressive of the organism as a whole. (pp. 31-2.)

Man has, then, to a very large extent lost touch with the warmth and solidarity of his total feeling-processes. He has attempted to force his feeling through partitive, symbolic channels. In this process it becomes distorted and issues as partitive feeling or affect. This partitive feeling is divisive to its core. It is displaced from its primary seat within the organism as a whole. It does not spring from the total organism and does not make contact with the organisms of others. It is thrown back upon one's symbolic concept or image of one's self and becomes centered upon what is good for Me and bad for Me.

Prejudice, or affect, always favors the "I," the isolated "I";

and this prejudice or affect is today the moving force of our lives. It is a socially active process that plays an unobserved but significant role in all man's interrelational difficulties. No one need be reminded of the hostility toward Jews and Negroes, or the suspicion and distrust between labor and management, or the divisive tendency of nationalism. Not many years ago our newspapers were full of admiring tributes to our noble ally Russia. That was affect, prejudice. Today our newspapers are full of accounts of the dastardly behavior of the same Russia. That, too, is prejudice. The basic behavior of Russia has not altered during the interim. Theodore Roosevelt and William H. Taft were fast friends all through Roosevelt's administration. Four years later no recrimination was too bitter for each to hurl at the other. I am profoundly irritated with my family on Tuesday, and on Thursday I am moved to tears at the contemplation of their devotion. All affect—all the social reflection of man's absorption in his image of himself and his vacillating self-advantage.

Group analysis was initiated, as has been said, with the aim of discovering a norm of human behavior that would be consistent, that would not vary with every changing wind of circumstance. But the specific data that led to the establishment of a biological norm as a basis of balanced behavior were not discovered for many years. Meanwhile the uncovering of a universal mood of affect and bias formed the center of the activity. The little essay that follows was written by a student who had witnessed the fierce antagonisms uncovered in the analysis of the group—a group composed of people who passed in ordinary life as unusually earnest, high-minded, and tolerant. She wrote the essay out of her sense of the hopelessness of all efforts to bring men together through concentrating on intellectual panaceas and leaving out of account the essential mood of oppositeness and competitiveness.

LE PETIT JEAN, HANSEL AND JOHNNIE

Mental and nervous disturbances in whatsoever form they may manifest themselves are not an isolated phenomenon of present-day civilization. Johnnie is a problem in his home and in his class room. Highly unstable, he is easily irritated and his tantrums almost invariably precipitate a quarrel between him and anyone who happens to come his way. Difficult though it may be to trace, there seems to be a perfectly logical connection between the squabble in which Johnnie becomes involved along with his little sister, his chum, his parents, his teacher or whoever it may be, and the most complicated economic or political situation in which any two great nations may become embroiled.

Johnnie knows that he is expected to make a good showing in his school work and among his companions socially. Otherwise he has to bear the burden of the chagrin his parents might suffer through the inability of their child to surpass his fellows. Johnnie is convinced of this—gentle though his parents may be toward him— for is not almost every boy in school fairly distracted with worry if he has to take home a report indicating failure, or else tremendously proud of himself if he can prove to his admiring mother and father that other parents do not possess such superior offspring as their own?

Johnnie knows that at home there is always a hope that he will stand at the head of his class. Before long he will want to be the captain of his football team, and after he graduates from college he must find a job that will make the other people in the world know what a superior chap he is.

But that is not all. Johnnie and his fellows are urged

to see to it that their school is "the best" in town, they are encouraged to make their summer camp "the finest" in the State, and above all they are made to understand that there is no doubt as to their country being "the greatest" in the whole world. It is therefore quite inevitable that any nation of Johnnies should face any other nation with a complete conviction of the perfect justice of the stand it may happen to take. Naturally, from this point of view each nation is merely standing face to face with a duplicate of itself, and there we are.

This state of affairs is of especial interest in view of the suggestion now being made to include in anti-war programs a sort of education in internationalism for young children. In large-looming ways and by high-sounding means the children are to be encouraged to think internationally. Surely there can be no objection to the aim in view. If le petit Jean can appreciate wholeheartedly the greatness of Goethe, if Hansel can accept without reservation the genius of Shakespeare, it is all so much to the good. But of what avail is this sort of thing if le petit Jean sees the pride in his mother's face because he is taller than Pierre two months his senior, if Hansel is praised by his father for getting the prize which Fritzl failed to attain, if Johnnie is acclaimed a hero because he happened to bloody Tommy's nose instead of letting his own eye be blacked?

J. B. S. Haldane tells us in a recent article that "until psychology is a science, scientific method cannot be applied in politics." Without doubt this statement holds good for international as well as for national politics. In the same article Professor Haldane refers also to the unwisdom inherent in the gentle art of prophesying. Nevertheless it is a tempting sport and the present thought invites indulgence in it. In the situation our prophecy runs somewhat thus. As psychology develops as a science there will inevitably be at the same time a change in what we now know as politics. For before the politicians of the coming years have reached the age of majority, the science of psychology will have thrown much light on the situation in which they are involved while they are still le petit Jean, Hansel and Johnnie.

The statement at the end of the foregoing sketch is of interest because it reflects the developmental stage of the experiment at that time (1925). It points to the need of a science of human behavior but envisages the problem only from a relatively limited psychological point of view. There was then no inkling of a method that would turn to the internal processes of man's organism for a solution of the problem.

The next sketch does not prophesy. It merely looks at the social reactions that grow out of affect.

"RIGHTEOUS INDIGNATION"

In all probability one could devote himself to no cause that would be less popular than an effort to disillusion ourselves of the notion that our indignation over the behavior of others is essentially righteous. A crime such as we ordinarily call dastardly is committed and a wave of emotion stirs the community to its very depths. The police force undertake an investigation, discover the supposed criminal to be completely irresponsible for his acts, he is judged legally insane and committed to an institution. The basis for our "righteous indignation" is completely undermined and it vanishes into thin air.

In these days of growing enlightenment as to mental states it is futile to attempt to deny the logical connection between an insignificant tantrum and the most heinous act of an irresponsibly insane criminal. To be sure they vary greatly in outward appearance, and from a practical point of view the measures to be taken by those affected in the two situations are necessarily completely different. But there is no man or woman so wise as to be able to identify the point at which normal mental functioning becomes unstable and again the point at which mental instability becomes noticeably pathological in character. And between the extremes here suggested there are represented conditions of every possible degree of shading.

This being true, there can be no one who is not included, from one point of view or another, in the very category at which each of us is wont to look askance as meriting our pity, our disdain, our fear or what not. The lowly outcast who hangs for the murder he has committed differs only in outward circumstances from the educated gentleman with all his refinement who from time to time loses himself in fits of ungovernable temper. The petty shoplifter in her station-house cell can be distinguished only by surface appearances from the woman of worldly culture who in ways so subtle as ordinarily to escape notice appropriates unto herself things that belong to others. No one of us can make good a claim that he does not represent the entire gamut of human characteristics and human possibilities. No one of us can look at any other without a realization that, given this, that or the other seemingly accidental change in his forbears or his upbringing, he and that other might have exchanged the worldly positions each of them now happens to occupy. So that likewise, in situations which do not involve a pronounced mental irresponsibility, there is equally no foundation for our "righteous indignation."

If I think I may claim for myself the privilege to stand off from you and criticize you, it is as though my right hand claimed to be more highly endowed than my left because it holds the pencil with which I am writing. It is from some such falsely assumed position of differentiation that there springs the criticism, the resentment, the sense of "righteous indignation" with the acts of others. Moreover we lay claim to warmth of feeling at a moment in which we are busily engaged in cutting ourselves off from our fellows, but this claim can be only a false signal to put us off the trail that is really ours. There can be no warmth of feeling accompanying a claim of betterness, of otherness, of separation. A withdrawal from human contacts is, of all our experiences, necessarily the coldest.

Consider for a moment any situation involving a show of "righteous indignation" which has come within the scope of your observation or indeed of your own experience. Boiled down, it will inevitably present some such picture as this. Jones has seriously offended Smith's sense of justice and the latter has become indignant— "righteously" so. Smith voices his emotion in no uncertain terms, and in response to this rejoinder Jones becomes indignant—"righteously" so. What is the net result? Two men, each indignant with the other, and each hugging to himself a false claim of "righteousness." The claims cancel out. Nothing is left.

How many of us at one time or another, overcome by the "stupidity" of our opponents, have said, "It's no use to argue. Nothing is ever gained by it." But does that statement keep us from arguing at the next opportunity? The underlying mood of authoritarian rightness remains untouched by any intellectual argument. We are married to our affects and must live with them.

THE CONSTANT ERROR

Before me is a letter and I read: "Please tell me frankly what you think of Dr. L. Do you feel about him and his work as you did four years ago?"

The query rouses memories. I see a man—a big man, talking; his head a little forward, his eyes shining, his whole figure tense with eagerness. He is a teacher, a dictator, an enthusiast. And those who listen to him are as tense as he. They are an instrument on which he has played until he is more sure of their response than of what he says. And he is certain of what he says. Standing beside him I, too, feel the certainty of what he says. I, too, watch his audience and glory in their assent. I see his eyes again and again sweep those before him, drinking in their unvoiced tribute. But I see, too, that he turns often to me who am beside him for the agreement and acclaim that I am so eager to express. I see him as a giant and myself as his pupil—his disciple—his protégé. Everything within my field of vision is dwarfed by this figure that I follow; everything is darkened by the shadow that it casts.

It so happened that about this time I went away, not freely but with a wrench.

The years slipped in between us and I saw him who had seemed a giant, as a human being and rather far away. Others who were nearer were larger than he.

And then—it seemed to happen quite naturally—I turned around, and he who had been a giant was gone. His shadow was no longer on the things I saw.

Before me is a letter and I read: "Please tell me frankly what you think of Dr. L." Words, phrases, and sentences surge into my mind as I take up my pen. I know so well what I want to write; the vivid graphic repudiation of my earlier enthusiasm, the ready defense of my present evaluation, the tolerant superiority for my former "views." I will write that it is I who have changed —that I have learned—that I am wiser now—that I have come to see those efforts (worthy enough, of course) from a broader viewpoint—that I could now teach him who once taught me.

But these things are not true.

I want to write that it is he who has changed; that he has lost his keenness—that he has not lived up to the promise that he gave. I want to criticize him for having gone backward while I went forward. I want to talk about his limited vision and the sterility of his effort.

But these things are not true.

My pen is in my hand and I write: "I do not know the man of whom you ask. At one time I saw a giant in his likeness but it was not he. And now I do not see him. Yet I am sure there is such a man. At one time he was in front of me and very close, so that I could not know him. Now he is behind me and rather far away. So that neither what I told you then nor what I would tell you now can be the truth. It is as though he and I had been on trains moving in opposite directions that had stopped side by side for a time at the same station. But now they are miles away. Yet I thought that what I saw then was true just as I think that what I see now is true. And because I do not see the man now as I saw him then I think that he has changed, or I, when it is

only my view of him that has changed—my position
toward him. I cannot see that change of position for I
am a part of it and I can see only from myself, outward.
I cannot know that I see only a fragment of life and
that fragment distorted, because I see only from myself,
outward, and because I can look in only one direction at
a time."

Affect, or the bias of wishful thinking, not only sets
brother against brother and nation against nation, it engenders
sloppy thinking and a general inertia even in the face of
horrible disease.

MENTAL SNAPSHOTS

People of righteous conscience are often heard to
remark sententiously that "they have no time for nerves."
Their position rests apparently on the view that nervous
conditions require leisure. They assume a fatal connection
between neurasthenia and luxury. In their minds nervous
prostration is inevitably linked with limousines, boudoirs
and a box at the opera. "Too much coddling" is the automatic verdict of these sturdy judges. "Let them go to
work; that will cure them," they affirm decisively. "I
didn't have any nerves when *I* was young. We never
even heard of nerves in my day. We had to get out and
hustle, we did." Thus with its unerring instinct for snap
judgments, the laity makes short despatch of the complex
problems of the sociologist and the psychiatrist.

This unenlightened attitude is deplorable enough
even among the illiterate classes in which it abounds.
Unfortunately, though, the uninitiated who declares
naïvely that idleness and ease are the cause of nervous
manifestations is too often sustained by the no less

illogical views of those who belong to presumably cultured ranks. Too often one hears from men of science an expression of view that is no more thoughtful or intelligent than the chance opinions casually passed by the average layman. But it is the men of scientific and literary culture whom one might expect to set the pattern of right thinking for the general community. It is to them that the layman would naturally turn in his effort to determine his own mental values. The inadvertence of the uninstructed layman is his failure to take into account all of the facts. But a census of the academic professions shows plainly that this scientific illiteracy is amply matched by a parallel tendency too often manifested in the so-called intelligentsia. If the unsophisticated fail to reckon in an inclusive sense with data bearing upon human motives and reactions, those among the presumably educated are no less reckless of the accepted canons of logic in their approach to these same human factors.

The layman in attempting to account for nervousness and insanity places ease and comfort in a definite causal alignment with these disorders. To make sure that his sum will come out even he must, of course, omit count of figures that do not tally with his preconceived values. He must, for example, confine his observations only to people accustomed to rich and idle surroundings. He must not reckon with the class of people whom circumstance has impanelled into an unremitting routine of hard daily labor. As if the overtaxed working woman, bending hourly under the burden of household chores and encumbered with a yearly increasing contingent of ill-nourished children, were not also to be rated high among the statistical percentages of insanity!

The truth is that in this fallacy itself there is precisely

the mental attitude that is responsible for nervousness and insanity; and this tendency to automatic and ill-considered judgments is precisely the basis upon which our aberrations of consciousness, individual and social, rest their support. Where such ineptitudes of judgment occur among men of science there is occasion for very serious challenge, and the conclusion is unavoidable that in their unwitting infringements of logic the mental processes of the literati keep steady pace with those of the unlettered individual. They too in their obsessive predisposition to have two and two make four quite fail to reckon on which side of the equation their values are found. As frequently as not they too are wholly unmindful that their terms may quite as often cancel out as yield the cherished quantity represented in their preconceived sum. The mere coexistence of phenomena is sufficient to warrant this type of mind in assigning a causal connection between them. In this logical fallacy there is embodied the identical method of reasoning that underlies the lay view. The layman observing two simultaneous conditions autocratically interjects a causal nexus. He arbitrarily infers sequence where there is a relation of mere coincidence. But such also are too frequently the transgressions of the academician and the scientist!

Is there not some latent confusion within the social mind generally that makes possible this tendency to unwarranted inference? Is there not some undiscovered—some as yet unaccountable—impulsion within the human mind that causes it to fashion proofs from the mere coexistence of phenomena? Since this fatal propensity is found alike in the cultivated and in the ignorant, is not this circumstance explicable only as the expression of an unconscious mass prejudice which in its limited outlook equally dominates the social perceptions of both?

Man has become like Ishmael, his hand against himself, his heart full of fear, his spirit perturbed with enmity. Every effort toward a more inclusive feeling is blocked by the mood of "me first" that motivates our accustomed affect and its way-ward projection. The story that follows is a firsthand account of a bit of affect-projection experienced by the writer himself.

I'LL GET MINE

What happened in the streetcar seemed at the time an experience quite peculiar to me. But I don't believe it was. I wonder if all of us aren't "tuned in," as I was, to pick up just such vibrations as I got. It wasn't the words. I hardly heard them. It was the voice. The words were something like this: "I'll get my ten dollars. I tell you I will. God! I'd kill that Eyetalian for ten dollars." I looked at the man. Anger and defiance in his face gave way to fear and self-pity. He began to whimper like a child. He spoke again, "Nobody cares what kind of a deal a man gets. No wonder men go to jail." Then with clenched fists, "I'll spend the rest of my life in jail but what I'll get my ten dollars. Him tellin' me what to do! I've been in that place twenty-one years and him twenty-one days and him a foreigner!"

I hardly knew that I was listening to this recital and yet as the man moved down the aisle of the crowded car I realized that I had responded to his outburst with intense emotion. In the moment I had developed quite definite delusions of persecution. I was ready to strike, and strike violently, at the individual responsible for my pain. I was afraid momentarily of punishment and social disapproval. I might be sent to jail. But didn't I know what was justly due me—ten dollars, or the life of a foreigner? And was not I supreme? What had society to do with me? I would defy the world and spend the rest of my life in defiance. I would be a martyr to the cause of justice. Didn't I know what was due *me*?

It came as quite a shock to me that this was my state of mind. Outwardly I was as composed as usual, but deep within I had vibrated to every play of feelings in a disgruntled workman. I looked at the people near me. Had they too responded as I had? Outwardly they were composed as I was. But I noted their tightly drawn lips, eyes hard and cold, expressions intent. There was among them no laughter, no warmth, no friendliness. Each was a stranger to the other. I have no doubt that each of them did feel just as I felt. That each one would get his ten dollars or kill a foreigner.

Here is affect rampant. No one in the streetcar is aware of the original situation that occasioned the anger of the workman. He himself is concerned solely with his hate. His attention has been deflected from the objective situation and centered entirely upon what seems to him to be an insult to his ego. Nothwithstanding the fact that nobody knows what it is all about, the entire group rises up in affective sympathy with the speaker. The writer is not only "tuned in" to the affect involved at the time of the incident, but we catch a note of it in his interpretation as subsequently expressed in the story. We feel with him that the workman is "a crazy fellow" who, for some mysterious reason, involved the author of the story in a mood to which he was not accustomed and which degraded him. But phylobiology makes clear that even before their encounter the writer's underlying mood of self-concern was identical with that of the workman.

Affect-projection by a community is pictured in the following story.

CHEATS

It happened in France when I was there last summer; in one of the smaller towns, Blois or Bourges, I forget which, and the incident took my interest because the girl in the story showed how impossible it is for one person alone, no matter how clearheaded or brave, to hold up the mirror to society, intrenched in its accepted hypocrisies.

There had been an examination held for some government positions—clerkships—just opened for women, and as the applicants returned to their homes several wore indignant looks and, with flashing eyes, declared that there had been cheating during the examination. One, more determined than the rest, took her complaint next day directly to the judge-advocate, called "le maître," who was final authority for that whole *arrondissement*. And thereby hangs a tale, for this man had secured his appointment in a way that had been an open scandal at the time, but since entering office he had been so strict that no one had dared breathe of the scandal. After some days of growing excitement, to please the complainants, a trial was announced.

"Le maître" presided. With all due impressiveness he presented the charges and indeed it seemed a serious situation; Mlle. Rabeau had been seen to cheat in a government examination. One by one the witnesses with varying expressions of indignation or virtuousness gave their testimony. There was no doubt about it, Mlle. Rabeau had cheated.

The judge summed up the testimony, paused and turned to the defendant, tensing himself for her outcry of defense. And here is where the thing happened. There was no outcry, no tears, no emotion. Mlle. Rabeau stood up, and I can see her muscular little figure now. In her clear energetic voice she spoke.

"I did cheat," said she, "I wanted the position and knew that if I didn't answer the questions I wouldn't get it, and I cheated. But I am no different from anyone here. Mlle. Carton," turning to the first witness, "you cheated me last week when I came to your shop and you sold me moth-eaten cloth, though you told me it had just come from the mills. And you, Mlle. Flournay," to the second witness, "showed the same thing a few days ago when I called at your house and you sent down word that you were out, for ten minutes later from up the street I saw you leave your house. And you, Mlle. Boulanger," to the chief witness, "are keeping to yourself a few adventures which you had last April in Le Havre. Sergeant Ravillon, who gave the examination, received a present of two hundred francs from a certain person the night before the examination." And turning to the judge, "*Monsieur le juge*, even you"— I saw the face of "le maître" suddenly become as putty—"perhaps even you can remember a time when you, shall we say, have cheated just a little."

There was a silence tense with feeling; not a word could anyone utter; even "le maître," usually so assured, sat there with knitted brows and studied the floor. Finally he pulled himself together and looked around the room. No one met his eye. He drew a deep breath and, "case dismissed," he uttered hoarsely.

That is where the story should have ended, but it didn't. Casual visitors in the town are still handled dishonestly at the Carton shop. The Mlles. Flournay are everywhere telling their social lies. Mlle. Boulanger still points to the motes in her sisters' eyes, and Sergeant Ravillon is guilty of taking bribes. But Mlle. Rabeau has been ostracized. No one knows her or her whereabouts any more.

Mlle. Rabeau is the one person on whom the others in the village, equally venal, could project their faults and heap criticism; the one person who was labeled "bad" and who was ostracized by those who had got by though they had committed crimes identical with hers. It is the old story of the "scapegoat" which the Israelites drove from their camp, vicariously carrying all their sins upon its head. We get a sense here of the fantastic basis upon which each of us preserves his secret conviction of being better than others.

Another essay presents various phases of affect-projection as noted in the early days of group analysis.

MENTAL OPTICS

Ordinarily we think that we see people clearly and interpret their reactions accurately; we may even pride ourselves on our facility in "character analysis."

But on studying our methods of observation, we see that one glance at someone gives us an impression which is either pleasant or unpleasant and that he reminds us of someone else. This means that our judgment is influenced by our association with previous situations and experiences, and hence our vision is governed by prejudice

for or against a person's appearance. Before we see someone, then, we are predetermined in his favor or in opposition to him.

Still more, however, is our observation invalidated by
our habit of projecting upon another person some un-
acceptable quality or reaction of our own, of which we are
not aware. We accuse the other person of having an
emotion which we really are feeling in ourselves. We can
have a "psychic blind spot" which prevents us from viewing in our own case what may be called a fault, but we
criticize this with extreme emotion when we think we see
it in someone else. In like manner we praise in another
those qualities which we secretly admire in ourselves.
We even go so far as to associate one person permanently
with the quality with which we happen to have invested
him, so that we call one person agreeable, another irritable;
but to maintain this impression in our minds we force
ourselves frequently to ignore the fact that the first person can at times demonstrate extreme outbursts of temper,
and the second illustrate on occasion infinite patience and
understanding. So when we attempt to study someone,
we really are but looking at a picture of that person we
have made up out of our own emotions.

In anger, perhaps, is our vision most distorted. In
this disturbed emotional state we indulge in the pleasure
of projecting all of our own disapproved reactions upon
the other person. We then think that we hate him and
wish to punish him, but really it is our image of the
person which we hate and desire to combat. Continuing
this tendency, we like to feel that our mood has arisen
solely because of the words or actions of the other. That
this is untrue is proved by the fact that, when we are
irritable, we feel it is caused first by one person, then

another until the situation takes in everybody we meet in the course of the day. So we cannot ascribe it to any one person as we had originally thought, but rather to our own condition of mind. And we are bent on following our "mental set" of the time being, as is shown by our unwillingness to relinquish this mood after all the objective conditions which brought on the disturbance have been removed or satisfied. We are more than loth to see that our moods arise within ourselves and that we are predisposed to an explosion when in the mood of irritability, much like a pile of gunpowder; that the words of the other person act but as the match to the waiting explosive. We are not able, or willing, to contemplate our volatile propensities.

The anger state has all the characteristics of insanity in that we are concerned only with a fantastic image of our own making which we have projected on the other person and, though partially aware of this, are really quite unwilling to think the image unreal. It was by no casual accident that the word *mad* came to mean both angry and insane.

The person whom we think we are observing is, on his side, doing just as we are doing; he is harboring a fanciful picture of us made up of his projections.

But we have been trained all of our lives not to see that the person we regard as other than ourselves is really identical with us, and the result of this artificial training is the basis of all those undependable misinterpretations which characterize our outlook.

Utilizing a social setting, phylobiology has demonstrated through innumerable observations that the misuse of the projective faculty is continual and universal. The projection upon

others of distorted feeling-processes has become the habitude
of us all. It can be observed in the casual social give-and-take
as well as in the intense flare-ups of affect. It underlies our
"normal" as well as our overtly pathological expressions of
possessiveness, jealousy, and hate.

The highly vaunted "in love" state is replete with affect-
projection. The long-standing yearning for home and security,
the endless procession of sexual fantasies that have hitherto
preoccupied the individual, now focus upon one object. The
lover projects his image of himself upon his loved one. He
fancies her to be the one person who has "the same interests"
and who "understands" him. She in turn projects her image
of herself on him, claiming him as "her other self." The
pseudopersonality of each is thus consolidated and receives
mutual affirmation. As long as each accepts the role assigned,
the relationship is outwardly harmonious. Indeed, it may continue unbroken throughout a lifetime. But let one or both step
out of character and fail to fulfill the role prescribed, and love
changes to hate. It was not by chance that the poet put into
the mouth of Juliet, his shining example of devoted love, a
scathing denunciation of her lover. "A damned saint, an
honorable villain!" she screams, on hearing that he has killed
her cousin Tybalt.

The appeal of soap operas, of the bulk of romantic novels
and the majority of motion pictures, is based upon the com-
pelling motivation of the projective mechanism. The fears,
the hopes, the repressed desires of readers and listeners focus
on the characters in the drama and thus receive vicarious
expression.

The outer symptoms of disordered feeling or affect-projection are legion. Affect-projection characterizes the behavior of
the seemingly dependent, unresourceful, infantile individual
as well as that of the outwardly aggressive, resourceful, domi-
neering personality. As we know, the individual who has been

conditioned to dependence tends to hold back, to evade responsibility, to desire to be ordered about. In his dissociation he projects upon others the responsibility for his attitude. In his disordered mood, he feels that others take advantage of him and "make him do" as they wish. He tries in roundabout ways to "get back at" those upon whom he has arbitrarily projected images of authority. Likewise the person who has been conditioned to aggression is equally lacking in internal balance and coordination—he is equally divorced from the feeling-processes of his organism. He inevitably justifies his ruthless tactics by blaming those about him for "standing in his way." The behavior of both types—no matter what the objective manifestations—is dynamically identical. Each claims that his antagonism, his oppositeness, is justified. This claim reflects the social compulsion under which we all labor to project our self-made images upon others.

This book is, of course, not concerned with the affect-projections of any one or any group of individuals. The stories presented in this chapter are illustrations of a malfunction that distorts the emotional responses of us all—teachers, preachers, psychiatrists, politicians, foreign ministers, United Nations delegates—high and low, great and small.

The essay now to be presented focuses attention upon a subjective reaction that is one of the curious phenomena accompanying the type of behavior we label "prejudice."

DR. FELL

I do not like you Dr. Fell
The reason why I cannot tell;
But this I know and know full well,
I do not like you Dr. Fell.

A friend of mine said to me the other day, referring to a mutual acquaintance, "Jack blankly refuses to read any of your stuff or to discuss your viewpoint from any

angle." "What seems to be the matter," I asked, "anything personal?" "Yes," answered my friend, "that's it
precisely—he just doesn't like you." "Come now," I said,
"that's a mere phrase." And then, in answer to my
friend's evident, though as yet unvoiced, objection to the
thought I had in mind, I said, "I know how frequently
we use this phrase and claim that it has some meaning
for us. But if you will consider for a moment what you've
said, you'll find there is no *real* state of mind corresponding to what you and Jack call his 'dislike of me.' You'll
find that it merely hangs in the air. Of course I realize
there is a state of mind underlying Jack's *apparent* attitude toward me, and it is that state of mind in which I am
interested. I feel that Jack must have in mind some
reason for not liking me, and it might help us if we could
know what it is."

"Well," said my friend, with growing irritation, "to
tell you the truth" (you see, as I suspected, he was only
beginning now to tell the truth) "he thinks you're self-
centered, socially oblivious and inclined to be disgruntled
toward the state of things in general." "But still I am
left in the dark," I said, "I can well understand his thinking these things of me. As a matter of fact he is quite
right. But what I cannot accept is a state of mind that
says of another 'I don't like him.' Not liking an individual
is a very uncomfortable feeling. I don't believe anyone
would encourage such sensations in himself had he any
understanding of what he was doing. I am sure that if
Jack would analyze his feeling, he too could not help
seeing how little he understands his own state of mind.
I am convinced that if he once looked at his state of mind,
he would find it exceedingly irksome.

"I remember there was a fellow at college whom I

cordially disliked. The very sight of this man stirred me to feelings of hatred and a desire somehow to punish him. That he was completely unaware of my attitude, or for that matter of my existence, did not in the least mitigate my aversion but rather intensified it. For the life of me I could not decipher my feeling at that time. I didn't dream that my dislike of Henry Markham was due to the fact that he was extremely good looking, which I was not, and that he was completely self-complacent toward life in general, while I was forever impatiently grubbing beneath appearances to discover, if possible, some clearer underlying meaning. Of course, in those days the deeper elements of an unconscious introversion did not enter into my calculations.

"That Jack should regard me as a social pariah, that he should believe that I am one of those people who holds himself to be the center of a system toward which all things converge and that he considers me in general a quite unadapted fellow, I quite understand. As I said, his criticism is in fact all very true. But a disagreeable, unprepossessing person like me, it would be thought, one would cast into the discard, efface, eschew, allow to drop out of the general vista of things. But Jack does nothing of the kind. On the contrary he is kept awake at night hating me. So strongly does his hatred of me attach him to me that he must be constantly making a supreme effort to go out of his way to avoid me. In other words, he must keep me diligently in mind in order to dispel me from his mind. This is a sorry contradiction and entails a most irritating impasse for Jack.

"I think it is just such mental and emotional factors as these toward which we fail to take an intelligent view. Our whole subjective sphere seems a quite dreary expanse of utter wasteland so far as any controlled and scientific penetration into the real constituents of its soil is concerned. I am sure that Jack, quite unsuspected by himself, is coerced into his attitude by the sheer force of some inherent claim upon me. And he must forever stand in his mental recess and, without my even being aware of him, look out on me with hatred as I pass. Such claims, I think, betoken always some innate bond. Says Rupert Brooke, 'For who decries the loved, decries the lover.' It is equally true, I think, that whoever directs his hatred outward directs it from a source of hatred unrecognized within. This hatred is the inner bond that cannot yield its claim. And so, would it not be well if Jack or you or I or any of us who is bound by the claims of such compulsive 'instincts' toward one another should look rather to the *bond* than to the *other* in his effort to account for his discomforting dissatisfaction? May it not be that Jack is also self-centered, that he too has a grudge against the habitual processes of life? May it not be that he too is socially as insulated from the warmth of generous human contacts as I appear from the angle at which he observes me? Is it unreasonable to ask whether Jack, after all, is not a victim of his own irreconcilable mental images, and to suspect that his attitude toward me is identical with that of my boyhood days toward my unoffending college mate? When we consider it, it is clear that if one dislikes some object around him—*really* dislikes it—he lets it alone. One does not voluntarily remain absorbed in the contemplation of an unpleasant sound or sight or smell. He instinctively thrusts it from him or he himself moves away. That is the natural reaction of any healthy organism toward an unpleasant or despised object. Does it not appear then that, where our reaction is so directly the contrary of this in respect to our human fellows, the object of such a human relationship is not foreign to us, that it is really not an *object* at all, not *really* a thing opposite us? Would it not seem rather that this manner of reacting indicates an inherently identical condition in us, and that what we have called the object opposite us is really the subject, the condition with which we ourselves are continuous?

"In this view, what we call our dislike is but our fascination with the image of our own selves. If this is true—and careful experiment would seem to indicate that it is—a wider knowledge and experience along these subjective ways of thinking and reacting might go far toward eliminating much of the conflict and disharmony in the social world at large. It might indeed set in operation a process of inquiry which, carried to its ultimate, logical end, would do infinitely more than all our elaborate planning to bring about terms of peace not only among individuals but among nations of individuals. Indeed it might even arrive at last at sensing the subjective causes that underlie the most serious of man's trespasses toward man. It might be that such a course of self-inquiry, were it wide enough in its extent, would at last eliminate the most outstanding of all our human reactions, namely insanity and war, based as they now are upon the automatic offensiveness of the fellow whom I assume to be other than *me* because he thinks and feels and acts not as *I* dictate he should think and feel and act. It might even be that, in sensing the hatred within, which now exists under the widespread social phantom of 'the other fellow,' man's social processes would seek world-wide expression in beneficent creativeness rather than in world-wide destructiveness and insanity."

As we look out at our world, with its inequalities of opportunity, its quarrels in home and office, its conflicts in industry and among nations—all shadowed by terror of the atom bomb—we necessarily feel that the most important task confronting man today is the study and understanding of his own behavior. But though we have an intellectual recognition of this need, we habitually avoid such a course of self-inquiry as is suggested in "Dr. Fell." We look with dread at the rapidly oncoming Third World War, but we do not recognize its prototype in our daily social gatherings, in our cherished family circles, in ourselves. It was the steady aim of group analysis to establish the problem of interrelational conflict as a problem internal to man's processes—to the processes of each of us. Its purpose was to study man's social reactions in the immediate moment and to free him from the affect-impedimenta which now clog his interrelational functioning. Such study and discipline is necessary if man is to bring to fruition his biological potentiality for social cohesion and integration. He would thus attain a freedom and coordination in feeling and behavior that far surpass our customary, "normal" experience.

CHAPTER IV

Social Conditioning

Reference has been made to the pseudopersonality developed in each individual through his conditioning in early childhood. In the Foreword to *The Neurosis of Man*, the report of his thirty years' research, Dr. Burrow says, "What man is overtly, is not what man is basically." The experiment of group analysis demonstrated over and over again that the so-called "personality" of a human being could be compared to a beleaguered castle with a series of defenses behind which lurked a frightened and bewildered child. It is not surprising, then, that much attention was given to the relation between children and parents and to the observation of a conditioning process that results in the kind of world in which we live.

A certain training, or conditioning, of the incoming generation at the hands of the adult generation is, of course, biologically essential. Naturally, children must learn to adjust themselves to their environment, physical and human. But, together with this objective training, we impose upon our children an affective conditioning that is insidious and destructive. We of the adult generation do not recognize the artificiality of this process because we ourselves have been similarly conditioned from infancy.

One of the most vital achievements of the young child is his mastery of language, his ability to manipulate symbols. Not only must he gradually learn the names of people and objects, but eventually he must also grasp the relation between certain symbols and certain experiences of his life. For example, he learns to associate the experience of stepping up with the word "up." When he tries to force a big object into a small container, the symbols "big" and "little" take on meaning for him. Such an application of symbol to actuality is of inestimable service to the child in his adaptation to the external environment. He gradually finds that symbols have a direct relation to his environmental setting, and he can test their validity by applying them to actual situations.

Phylobiology calls our attention to another set of symbols the learning of which bulks large in the education of every child. These symbols have to do with the moral dichotomy of "right" and "wrong." They have nothing to do with the biological stimulus and response involved, for example, in such self-training as learning to differentiate between hot and cold, or learning to handle glass objects differently from wooden objects. On the contrary, they are connected with a mysterious and immanent mood-entity called "right" or "good." If the child does "right" he gains the approval of his parents and teachers. If he does "wrong" he loses their approval. The "love" they are constrained to offer him is not a simple continuity of feeling between them and him. Their love is self-conscious. It is shot through with affect—with sentimental possessiveness or overanxious solicitude, with personal irritation or self-centered pride. Its medium of exchange is approval and disapproval. But the child's most insistent need is to fulfill his sense of oneness with his kind. Denied this, he must perforce accept the counterfeit in lieu of the real thing. So that the striving-for-approval ("goodness") or the repudiation-of-approval ("badness") becomes the mainspring of his behavior. He has been diverted from biological incentives to moral incentives. He has learned to posture before his community.

In our haste to be "right" and to tell children what they should do we leave out of account the fact that in our present social and educational setup our judgments have been handed down to us preformed. The motivation we inculcate in the younger generation has been given us secondhand. Moreover, the artificial standards of "good" and "bad" we handle so glibly have no solid basis anywhere, but change with the passing mood or convenience of the person who holds up this variable yardstick to the child's behavior. The symbols of "right" and "wrong" we teach him are mental images that have no counterpart in the world of reality. Our "normal" behavioral right and wrong do not make contact at any point with what is biologically fitting or unfitting. The meaning of these symbols changes from person to person, from situation to situation, from time to time. The only immutable feature of this symbolic "right" is that it is ever synonymous with self-advantage. We thus equip the child for his journey through life with fluctuating values and transitory precepts rather than with dependable charts and compasses.

Most important for students of behavior is the phylobiological finding that a spurious image of the self, composed of a cluster of affects, is forced upon each individual child by the adult generation. An artificial, moral interdiction blocks the child's wholesome biological impulse to explore all phases of his environment—gadgets, bric-a-brac, his sex organs and those of his playmates, as well as the causes and relations of much that he sees. Quickly his interest to investigate comes up against what to him are utterly mysterious barriers. Certain areas are forbidden and must not be explored. The implication

is that he may not share the secrets of those Olympians, the
adults. Through repeated impressions upon his receptive spirit,
he is compelled to believe that his "bad" behavior and even
his "bad" thoughts are different from those of his parents, and
that it is safer not to talk about those things with them. Even
if there is an attempt at communication, adults can speak to
a child only out of their own conditioned, moralistic mood.
And it is to this mood that the child reacts, not to the words.
Continuity of feeling between himself and his fellow human
beings has been interrupted. Gradually he comes to feel that
he is special and apart. He learns to be tricky and becomes less
capable of direct feeling. "Right" and his own self-interest
are now identical. Henceforth he is motivated by pseudo-
feeling or affect.

Perhaps the two stories that follow will throw some light
on the process in which "right" is right in one setting and not
in another, depending on the advantage to be gained. The
utter falseness of such prompting to behavior is a mortal
affront to the organic integrity of the child.

BEING GOOD

Not many weeks ago I had dinner with a friend, and
as a special favor to her young son the meal hour was
arranged so that he could be at the table with us. It was
probably the unusual social gaiety that kept him awake
long after he was accustomed to be asleep, and his mother
and I were interrupted by frequent calls from his bedroom.
Finally his mother went to him and as she left the room
I heard her say gently, "Now Billy be a good boy and
turn over and go to sleep." Somewhat apologetically she
said to me, "I don't ordinarily go to Billy when he calls,
but this evening I thought you might find him annoying."

The incident was insignificant enough to be sure,

and probably it would have disappeared completely from my mind had it not been recalled shortly after by another, in itself equally insignificant. On this occasion another mother was on her way home, with two children, from what must have been a burdensome shopping expedition. They had to board a crowded streetcar, the mother carrying the baby and a basket and keeping her eye on the small girl behind her. The older child was evidently exhausted by the trip, and she had no sooner settled comfortably in her seat than her little head began to nod threateningly. With one despairing glance that took in basket and baby and sleeping child, the mother shook her and said, "Oh Mary! Do be a good girl and keep awake."

As the two incidents established an association in my mind I found myself distinctly puzzled. Here were two children called on to face a moral issue—each one asked by his mother to be "a good child"—and one was to meet the issue by going to sleep, the other by keeping awake. If I was puzzled, what of the two children? What of any one child who, it is easily conceivable, might be called on to play the principal role in both situations? Was there really a moral issue involved, I asked myself, or was this not rather a camouflage whereby the mother could gain her end more comfortably? In each instance there was a mother inconvenienced by her child, the one by a child who stayed awake, the other by a child who went to sleep. Neither mother could overcome the inconvenience alone, and the cooperation of the child was not easy to gain. Quite unknowingly therefore, it seemed to me, each mother found herself forced to offer her child a bribe, and this bribe was her mother love. Subtly she said "Bill—or Mary—if you will do the thing that will make me more comfortable, then I will call you a good child and you will have my love." And safe in the possession of the greatest possible prize a child can gain—its mother's love—Billy went to sleep and Mary stayed awake.

Quite automatically after that I found myself on the lookout for similar situations. I knew that what had happened with Billy and Mary must be happening with other children, but probably so subtly as to escape attention. I had not long to wait for further enlightenment.

Conspicuous in the church-going community in which I live is Mr. Owens, an ardent believer in the teaching of Ingersoll. Mr. Owens' son Buck stopped at my porch one afternoon with his friend, Tom Griffin, whose parents are very earnest in their attendance at church. The boys began to talk about their personal affairs, and an occasional question on my part brought out the very information in which I was interested. Tom, quite naturally it would seem, is expected to go to Sunday school regularly, and in moments of mutiny he has been told that "all good boys go every Sunday." At such times he is, also quite naturally, envious of Buck's apparent freedom, but is the freedom real? Buck, attracted by fruit forbidden on pain of serious punishment, sneaked off on one occasion and went to Sunday school with Tom. I quote his own statement as to what followed discovery of his whereabouts. "When Dad found out where I'd been he gave me a lickin' and 'deed Miss I don't know yet what it's all about."

Once more, it seemed to me, there was the same thing in slightly different form. The implication of morality —of "being good"—in behavior that conforms to the family standard, and the reverse when it does not.

Again I found my porch on a summer afternoon a most profitable listening post. On this occasion a bloody altercation had taken place in my neighborhood, and the excitement had drawn me to the scene. In spite of efforts to remove the signs of battle, Joe Clark and Nick Crothers, the principals in the affair, went home, the one with a bloody nose, the other with a swollen eye. The next afternoon the two boys, now reconciled, wandered by and rather sheepishly responded to an invitation to visit me. Both boys were disobeying strict orders from home by being together, for Joe's mother had told him that Nick was a bad boy whom he must not associate with, and Nick had been similarly warned concerning Joe.

Unprejudiced by a maternal solicitude that singled out either Joe or Nick, they looked pretty much the same to me. Each mother therefore, I thought, in issuing her warning against association with "a bad boy," was hugging to herself the illusion that her son was "a good boy." And in this situation it could mean only that through some distortion of self-flattery each mother had so juggled the term "my child" as to make it mean for her "a good child." I found myself wondering how Mrs. Brewster would have disposed of the issue of "goodness" and "badness" if her twin sons had disfigured each other in the same way that Joe and Nick had done.

In spite of these comparatively trivial incidents there is involved a question of vital importance. Do the children suspect—and more important still—do we grown-ups suspect the self-deception in which we are all involved? The question merits our most earnest consideration.

THE CROSSROAD

Ethel was on the sofa, busy with her doll and her kitten, while Ethel's mamma—as a good hostess should—was telling me something I "mustn't mention."

"Of course we couldn't possibly go," she said to me, "and so I just told her that we were going to be out of town."

Ethel turned around on the sofa and her feet dropped over the edge. "Told who, Mamma?"

"Mrs. Brown, dear."

"But we weren't out of town!"

"I know, Ethel, but I had to tell her something."

"But, Mamma, isn't that a lie?"

"I suppose it is very much like a lie. But we couldn't go, Ethel, and I couldn't tell her why we couldn't go and I had to tell her something!"

"But it *was* a lie, Mamma, and you've said—"

"I know, but sometimes there are things that Mamma has to do!" Then, rather pointedly to me, "Have you been down to the art exhibit?"

Ethel's rigid little figure loosened a bit as the conversation continued to exclude her. After a time she went back to her kitten and her doll.

Back in the childhood of each one of us—when we were little Ethels and Marys and Johns—we came one day to a crossroad. It was not the first. The first crossroad was very long ago before our great-great-grandparents were little Ethels and Marys and Johns—so long ago that the story has become easy with much retelling. To the child mind came dimly the sense that there were two ways; that along one road lay the world as the child mind knew it, but the crossroad was "Mamma says." And because the two were not the same there was confusion and distress. If "Mamma says" were the right road, then the world as the child mind knew it must be wrong. It is hard to deny the world one knows. But on the other hand, if the child's world were right, then Mamma would be wrong. And Mamma couldn't be wrong! That seemed obvious. "Mamma says" sounded safe and sure, and the child in his own unsureness turned his back on the world as he knew it to follow "Mamma says." Not once, but again and again and again. A thousand times the child mind met the problem and a thousand times the child mind turned. Until the turning was a reflex—automatic and predictable and sure. But with that turning, the world as the child mind knew it disappeared—all but a half-forgotten memory. The reality of the world was lost, and with it was lost the simple sincerity that is the birthright of everyone.

The feeling of the race of man, channeled as it is into such fictitious courses, has become muddied with dark and alien accretions. Even the seemingly benign behavior of a mother toward her child is tinged with the mood engendered by her own affective conditioning. Children reflect the disordered social mood much more than we commonly recognize.

The following essay, written for *Mental Health* in 1923, is a forthright challenge of much that we consider sound in our methods of training children.

TRAINING

A child's earliest experience begins with social interdiction and command. His first lesson consists of rules pursuant of policies *for* or *against*. At every moment he is confronted by a choice between two courses. The one is good and must be followed, the other is bad and must not be followed. To discover which is which he can only consult his system of rules. In this wise the child's entire consciousness comes to be based upon division, alternative, *right* or *wrong*. This dual premise becomes coterminous with his every outlook. No act, no thought is exempt from its interference.

Every individual is thus the incarnation of extraneous codes and conformities. His conduct does not arise from his spontaneous feeling, but is artificially induced by the exactions of outer precept and ordinance. Instead of a free and harmonious individual, he becomes a carefully gauged mechanism. Instead of a medium of natural expression, he is subject to impediments and substitutions foisted upon him by his social environment. Compelled to learn by rote this catalogue of rules and observances, he must be prepared at all times to collate his behavior with the given circumstance and act in accordance. For with the constant enforcement of adjustments from without, all spontaneity from within is precluded. "What will others think of me?" is the mental attitude instilled by this self-conscious system of training. "What ought I to do in such and such a circumstance?" the child is taught to ask himself. All of us labor under the exacting demands of a social order that prompts us to ask, "How do other people act under such conditions? Shall I be approved or shall I be blamed?" The burden entailed is onerous. The demands are unrelenting, and under the strain the individual finds himself fretted, curtailed, self-critical. With his growing sense of self-depreciation, it is an easy step to the attitude of suspicion and fear that is the beginning of mental or nervous breakdown.

We have paid too little heed to the influence of this social dictatorship with its arbitrary control of the reactions of childhood. We have had too little regard for this factor of mental and social repression and its effect upon the nervous organization. Accustomed to view nervous processes only from the limited standpoint of the individual, we fail to recognize the responsibility of the social environment toward these disharmonies. We little realize to what extent the individual is hedged about and restricted by the numerous obstacles to individuality which the manifold covenants of the social body have constructed about him. These obstacles to the spontaneous expression of personality are called "training" but we fail to recognize the widely prevalent implication of such social inhibitions and to count their cost among the factors that lead to nervous and mental disorders.

Another comment stresses the inevitable recourse to subterfuge forced on the child by the community's endorsement of cunning and secrecy in its interpersonal relations.

THE MENACE OF THE NURSERY

To inculcate in the mind of childhood an early conflict of feeling is to occasion an organic discrepancy from which there is seldom, if ever, the possibility of recall. Every child looks to "Mother" as the embodiment of all that is good. From her he first learns the nature of goodness and how it must be discriminated from what is bad, and thus it is from Mother that he learns the law of his behavior. It happens, however, that the law of the nursery is not consistent. It does not fit all circumstances. It does not measure up to all occasions. Willie learns from the nursery code that a nice, good little boy does not have dirty fingernails, that he does not eat soup noisily or talk with his mouth full. But Willie observes that Uncle Joseph is the shining exponent of all these inadvertencies. Not only must Uncle Joseph noise it abroad whenever he eats soup, not only does he talk with his mouth full and overflowing, but to Willie's inexpressible disgust Uncle Joseph has the unpleasant habit of seizing impulsively upon Willie at just such times and covering his face with lax, voluptuous kisses. Willie shrinks miserably from these vulgar assaults of Uncle Joseph's. Everything within him rises up in protest against these affronts to his private feeling. Mother's image of Uncle Joseph and his own distressing impression of him are not reconcilable. This puzzles Willie. He does not understand. In Mother's eyes, of course, there is really no discrepancy at all. Willie simply fails to realize that Uncle Joseph is Mother's bachelor uncle and very rich. Indeed Willie's older brother, Joseph, has been named after Uncle Joseph. For poor Mother has never been able to have all the things that she wanted and secretly hopes to inherit Uncle Joseph's wealth. But Mother doesn't tell Willie all this. She hides this from him as from herself, as she must hide it also from Uncle Joseph, whose ill manners would be intolerable to her but for her expectations of future gain. But Willie feels that Mother is so good and would not tell a story for anything. And yet here before him stands a blatant story. Willie just does not understand. It cannot be so, and yet so it is. That is why Willie is puzzled.

As Willie grows older he comes into contact with other nursery products like himself, and with them he now cunningly connives in maintaining the code of secrecy and pretense that was the early training of their nurseries. Willie feels that there is a contradiction everywhere, a diplomacy, a falsehood, a subterfuge; but no one must speak of it. And so Willie is soon as completely won over to the adult syndicate of pretense that now surrounds him, as he was won over to the secret consensus of pretense that underlay the policy of his nursery training. It is a condition he must never speak of, not even to himself. His lips must remain forever sealed as in the days of his earliest childhood, and for precisely the same reason now as then, namely, that he would offend Mother, and Mother is the embodiment of goodness.

Thus out of the confederacy that was the nursery of one's childhood a larger confederacy is formed in adult life. Educated under the menace of nursery rules and regulations this secret corporation flourishes still in later life where, under the same pretense of an outer code of behaviorism, it grows into the confederacy of normal adulthood popularly called society.

In the portrayal of bewilderment and pain that follows, the child is speaking from behind the barrier of self-protection and "rightness" we force upon him. He has joined the confederacy of "good" and "bad" which we adults mistakenly feel is the basis of life. This snapshot also discloses through the child's eyes the insecurity of the puzzled, adult generation, due to their conditioned preoccupation with the evanescent standards of "good" and "bad."

FUNNY THINKIN'

Yestiddy I went to spend the night with Jack. Jack 'n Grace 'n Polly 'n me had lots o' fun. Least we did at first. We was havin' a piller fight, that was more fun! We got awful hot pumm'lin' each other, so we took our nighties off. That's more fun yet, rushin' 'round 'n feelin' there's nothin' on you to stop you from runnin' 'n jumpin'. I love the feelin' o' differnt things on m'self too. The piller, it was smooth 'n cool, Polly's hair it felt nice 'n soft, and Jack's breath it was hot and puffy. Jus' as we was skippin' 'n twirlin' 'n havin' the most fun of all, the door came open awful quick and sudden.

Jack's mother she looked awful funny and her face was real red. She was awful mad 'n cross. We all had to get real still. Sumpin' seemed like t'was gonna happen. Then Jack's mother, she put Polly's nighty on so quick 'n looked so scared I had to wonder why. I couldn't o' wondered why if she hadn't made a why for it, could I? It sets me thinkin' again awful. I never seen nothin' o' Polly 'n Grace till she came in. They was just like Jack 'n me. We wasn't thinkin' 'bout each other, only playin'. Now I has to think o' Polly 'n m'self 'n why 'n skins 'n— Gosh!

Ain't Polly's skin good? An' ain't it pretty? Ain't it jus' like Jack's? Ain't it hers what she was born with? Seems like if we was used to seein' skins 'n things just as we growed from the beginnin' nobody 'd think nothin' 'bout it. Just like we sees trees 'n animals 'n things. Ev'rybody looks at 'em and thinks they're butiful and don't fuss none 'bout coverin' 'em up. I wonder how it is that grownups just got to make you take notice o' sumpin' that don't make no difference 'n all the time they says it does, and makes you think you think it. Don't they put sumpin' in your head doin' that? Seems when people points out things 'n makes 'em speshul they just gets speshul. You has to begin to think of 'em. Seems like they ain't real important—they'se just part o' you or part o' what you do. Ev'rything seems so awful 'portant to grownups. They'se the scaredest people! They'se all the time scared. They'se scared you'll get cold, they'se scared you'll get hot, they'se scared you'll get burnt, they'se scared you'll get hurt—and most of all they'se scared you'll see sumpin' or say sumpin' or do sumpin'. Seems like people's got funny ways o' thinkin' 'n they keep right on with that funny thinkin'!

The same process is pictured in the next piece, from a somewhat different point of view.

MAMMY 'PINIONATES

I hears folks sayin' all 'round, "I jest never kin trust dese here chillen o' mine anywhar! They's always huntin' trouble. If I ain't dar to head 'em off, they ain't no tellin' what they'll do." I ain't gwine to 'cept no legacy like dat fur my chile—no suh! *I* says, "Little chillen sure is got a heap o' sense!"

Dese folks says little chillen ain't got no sense 'bout takin' keer o' theyselves. They ~~~ys chillen don't know whar danger is and whar it ain't. Lor' honey! ain't dis why? Folks never 'lows chillen a chance to try fur they-selves. 'Peers to me like little chillen's *mighty* smart. Folks kin be watchin' out fur 'em to see what's gwine to happen, but they don't need to head 'em off fust, do they, befo' nothin' happens? Ain't *no* chile kin larn nothin' dat way.

Most folks I sees dat reckons they's helpin' is mostly hinderin'. Is you ever seen 'em helpin' chillen to walk? 'Peers like little chillen's so wobbly, they needs *all* they-selves to help keep stiddy. 'Stead o' dat, folks reckons they has to pull on to they arms turrible. They near about yanks 'em offen de groun'. You sure ain't spectin' no chile to larn to walk 'ceptin' he larn hisself. And he sure cyarnt larn hisself 'ceptin' he carry hisself along.

I says, "Little chillen sure is got sense." I took my chile down in de garden whar de pond is, and whar it's good and warm and sunny. I knows he is gwine to make towards dat water soon as he kin, and I jest says to myself, "I'se gwine to see what dis here chile's gwine to do if I jest leaves him be." I was bound fur to see how he'd do, if I ain't doin' nothin'. Sposin' he went splashin' in dat water, I ain't gwine to do nothin' 'ceptin' pull him out arfterwards! So sure 'nough, he makes towards dat pond befo' you wink you eye. I ain't sayin' nothin'. When he gits to de aidge, he 'peers kinda keerful like. I take hold o' dat chile's dress, jest light, so's not to skeer him off none. He don't know I'se dar. I clar to goodness I'se sartney 'lowin' fur him to fall in dat pond! He bring his two little foots together clear on de aidge, and he swayed 'round mighty unsartin. I'se speculatin' what's gwine to happen! *Lor' honey!* he sway out, but bless you, he right hisself direc'ly. Den what you reckon he done? He backs hisself off jest as keerful like as you please—fust one foot, den de other, twel he gits away. Presen'ly he goes off playin' by hisself jest like nothin' ain't 'sturbed him.

I'se purty sure now dat chile reckons 'bout fallin' or not fallin' in ponds. 'Peers to me if I hada obstruc' dat chile from dat water, he is sartney got a right to git mad, 'cause he's out fur seein' what he kin see. 'Peers to me, if I cotched him while he's unsartin, it'd make a heap o' difference—'cause he done it hisself. I knowed little chillen's got a heap more sense den what folks says they is. *Lor' honey!* ain't I tell you? I ain't gwine to 'cept no legacy like dat fur my chile—no suh! How's chillen gwine to 'monstrate dat sense to folks if folks don't never give 'em no chance?

Again we have the child interpreted by a sympathetic adult.

SALLY

It is a lovely afternoon and as I walk along thinking of the events of the morning, Sally is skipping by my side. We come to a beautiful green slope and Sally throws

herself upon the grass in great glee. I think, "What fun
it is!" But suddenly the sense of communion I feel is cut
short. I am conscious of a presence close by. It is that
of a lady. The atmosphere about her is vibrant with
criticism. It says—"Isn't this dreadful! I have never
seen such behavior! What is the woman thinking of—
letting her child roll around in that way!" Immediately
I am of the atmosphere. The rigid mouth and formidable
front of disapproval convey themselves to me like an
electric current. I try to think—"Perhaps she means that
the grass is wet? Or that Sally's coat may be spoiled? It
is certainly one in which to play, however. What then
does the woman mean?" Of course it is Sally's behavior,
and I automatically become ashamed.

We have almost forgotten the formidable lady in our
endeavor to cross the street, but there we meet Mrs.
Bangs. (Sally is busily engaged in counting the number
of red and blue spots on an advertising sign which I know
to be most engrossing.) In the ensuing conversation of
Mrs. Bangs and myself there is something in her allusion
to Sally that savors of disapproval. I try to think, "Sally is
no doubt finding out something that interests her and
does not heed Mrs. Bangs and myself, but she is certainly
quite all right. She is not interfering with our conversation
in any way so it is not that that displeases Mrs. Bangs.
She has not the manners she should have—that is it!"
Again it is Sally's behavior. Again I find myself very self-
conscious in regard to Sally—I have fallen in with Mrs.
Bangs' mood also.

On the way home Sally has lost some of her vigor and
gaiety. Why not? Has she too caught the formidable
look of the lady or the disapproving tone of Mrs. Bangs?
If not, she has caught the self-conscious look I wear.

I am sure Sally is set again to wondering. It is not the wondering of "What fun!" She wonders, "Is it I who displease them? What must I do or what must I not do? What must I say or what must I not say? When Mrs. Bangs is cross must *I* have to do something? If Mama looks queer do *I* have to say something?" And so Sally must wonder all day long. She is set to wondering so much and so many days about why this and why that in regard to behavior, that little of the real Sally has time or zest to think, "What fun!"

A SKETCH

A mother sits down to the table with her child. She is very solicitous of his appetite. She watches every motion. She makes every motion for him. She encourages him to eat. She wishes him to eat certain things. She warns—she scolds—she threatens.

She is very solicitous of his appetite.

A child sits down to the table with his mother. He has no appetite. He cannot eat. He knows she is solicitous of his appetite. He knows also he does not have to move. She will tell him to, or she will move for him. Unwittingly he spontaneously finds something he wants and starts to eat.

He must not eat *celery*—he must eat *peas*. She wants him to eat yet she will not let him! He does not understand. He does not eat—he cannot eat—he has no appetite. She scolds, she threatens.

She scolds because he is not hungry. He does not understand why he is naughty because he cannot eat.

His mother is solicitous of his appetite.

She watches every move.

The child has no appetite.

The reader must bear in mind that all of the stories were written by students who were just beginning to be interested in Dr. Burrow's broader outlooks as these developed through his research work. It will readily be sensed that, for all their sensitive appreciation of the pain and frustration children suffer, the sketches we have just been reading are limited in their mood-outlook. The author quite obviously identifies herself with the child and thus inevitably falls a prey to a sentimental mood. She ignores the fact that with children as well as with adults the sense of right has become identified with one's personal advantage.

The theme of childhood frustration is developed in a more objective manner in the following essay.

CHILDHOOD

Whatever the condition, it must be taken for granted. One wants to know why, but one must not ask. If it is so, that is sufficient reason. One must never ask why. And whatever you do, you must not ask Mama. If Mama says it is so, it is so. A nice little boy or girl wouldn't *think* of asking why (italics Mama's). And if you are naughty and persist, you will just have to wait and ask Papa when he comes home. . . . At last Papa comes home but he is too tired now. I wonder if Mama knew he would be too tired when he came home. If she— but this is asking why again. Besides, Papa says "Children should be seen and not heard." He means, I suppose, they mustn't be heard asking "why."

After a while one gets very much a sense of being cut off by this "naughty" way he has of asking questions. Has he not been told how naughty it is? He begins to feel very much alone, but he feels that loneliness is the only recourse of naughtiness. Soon naughtiness and loneliness come to be one and the same thing in the mind of

a child. This sense deepens, and since one must not ask
why—must not even think why—gradually one begins to
have fancies all one's own. Of course fancies all one's own
are the unavoidable result of not being permitted to share
the thoughts of other people. But childhood does not
know these things. It must not know them, for that too
would be asking questions. After a while the fancies of
childhood begin to burrow in. They get further and
further below the surface. These secret fancies of a child
come slowly to form the very fabric of his being. For
since question, thought and the-reason-why belong to
older people, older people *know*. Mama and Papa have
said so. And Mama and Papa are all of childhood's world.

In his naughtiness, in his loneliness, the child becomes
more and more isolated in the world of his own fancies.
Gradually, in his growing need for self-comforting he falls
into the way of *doing* things that are equally naughty.
He feels this. He feels that what he does is naughty, that
it is sick and unfit. Something tells him so. He wishes
he didn't do it. He wonders why he does. But, of course,
he mustn't ask why. That would be naughtier than—
than—and besides if he asked why, Mama and Papa would
know how naughty he was to ask why, since they had told
him not to—and Mama and Papa are all of a child's world.
Do Mama and Papa ask each other why, he wonders. But
again it is naughty to wonder whether Mama and Papa
ask each other why.

It is clear that all of a child's world is a closed world.
He doesn't know, he doesn't suspect the truth—that the
world of his parents is a closed world too, that the world
of older people is full of loneliness, naughtiness, of fancies
and secret deeds of which they dare not inquire what is
the meaning—about which they dare not ask why. Child-

hood does not know that both Mama and Papa left the
homes of their parents and came to live together in their
own home precisely because together they had agreed
that they would not ask why, that together they would
accept what *their* parents had together taught *them*—
that one must not ask why.

I once knew a child who asked his parents why God
had made him and why he had been told in church
that he must be grateful to God that He had made him.
His mother said he should be grateful to God for having
given him his life because God had prepared a home of
everlasting happiness for him if only he would be good.
"If only"— The child shuddered, remembering his secret
fancies and his secret deeds. But, daring once more to
venture upon the way of reason, he asked had not God
also prepared hell for him if he were not good? And the
mother replied: "You must not talk like that, that is
naughty." But that was just why the child did talk like
that. He knew already that he was naughty, that he was
alone, that his world was a closed world and that by its
logic of loneliness and sin it was leading him inevitably
into this place they called "hell."

He was naughty then, and now he is insane. The hell
that was the logic of his closed world has closed in upon
him, because he asked questions, because he ventured
into the closed world of his parents and of his parents'
parents. He did not know that all the world is a closed
world. He did not know that the closed world of his
mother could not anywhere make contact with the closed
world of her child. He was naughty, but then (and this
must never be told) his mother was naughty too. For
was not she, too, confined within the secret world of
fancies in which the naughtiness of her childhood had

from her earliest years confined *her?* Had not she, too, been bound by the same social covenant to the same secret fetish that one must never ask why? And so the hell that is the logic of the child's closed world has its counterpart in his mother too. If his is a closed world, the world of his parents is equally shut in.

Must man ever remain under the thrall of this secret childishness and repression? May he not take reckoning of his slow, age-long descent and come to recognize, from patient examining, how his life everywhere abounds with superstitious fancies and impressions that shut him out from his rightful estate of thought? May not man, alone, supported solely by the strength of his own mind, face about and, uniting his strength with the united strength combined of his own and other men's thought, confront this closed world of their common childhood with its loneliness and its secret fancies? May he not replace the social medium composed of their common fancies and their fears with the saner medium of their common thought? Only in this wise—only in the strength of his social unanimity and fearlessness of mind will man at last throw open the closed world of his repressions and concealments to the clear light of reality and so dispel the hobgoblin of secrecy that marks still the childhood of our race.

The four stories that follow are likewise sympathetically concerned with the impact of grownups upon children. They were all written by one student and, as we shall see, reflect her shy and sensitive personality.

"HENRIETTA COPY-CAT"

"And we have a club—all the girls in my class are in it—and we have pink ribbon badges with fringe. And once we had a party, with ice-cream and chocolate cake. . . ."

The lively little girl across the aisle, who had been bored almost to tears by the railway journey with an unresponsive uncle, had at last found a listener, and was pouring forth a flood of pent-up conversation to the young lady opposite.

"And the motto of our club," she ended, with a flourish of trumpets in her voice, "is 'Henrietta Copy-Cat'!"

The young lady pricked up her ears. The "motto" had a rhythmic swing. She could imagine it being chanted in a loud sing-song by a chorus of children. Somewhere in this paradise of pink ribbons and ice-cream there was a victim.

"Who is Henrietta?" she inquired, as innocently as possible.

"Oh, *Henrietta*"—the child's voice vibrated with scorn —"she's just a *norful* little girl with red hair. She's in our class, and she's the only one who isn't in the club. You ought to see her—her clothes are *fierce!* And she keeps on tagging after us, and *tagging* after us, and trying to do everything we do, so our motto"—the child giggled—"is 'Henrietta Copy-Cat'."

The young lady thought for a moment. For a while, in her childhood, she had been in Henrietta's shoes. It was not an experience to be forgotten easily.

"Don't you think," she began, tentatively, "that maybe it's a little hard on Henrietta to be the only child who is not in your club? And she can't help having red hair. Perhaps it makes her unhappy when you laugh at her."

There was a moment's silence. One could almost hear the machinery creak in the child's mind as she hastily reversed the gears to avoid a collision with grown-up disapproval. Then she burst out, stammering in her eagerness to be "in the right" once more—

"Oh, but the *real* motto of our club—the really *truly* motto—is 'Do unto others as you would they should do unto you'!"

This is not merely a funny story. It illustrates a tendency which forms the basis of such tragedies as war or insanity. Henrietta was considered "different." She wore queer clothes, she had red hair, therefore she was not considered to be a human being. She was legally fair game, and could be hunted, and denied her share in the communal life of other children. Such ostracism and persecution might very easily result in serious or irreparable damage to the mental health of a sensitive child. When one is young and lonely it is impossible to see the group consensus of opinion in true perspective. One simply cannot believe that one's contemporaries are not "in the right," though in truth they may be merely voicing conventional prejudices. A child like Henrietta will instead believe that there is something innately repulsive and wicked in herself. She will go around in terror of giving offense, with growing suspicion that other people hate her and are trying to harm her. Or else she may withdraw entirely into her dreams, and cease to try to make any contact with reality.

Perhaps we may some day come to realize that this delusion of a "difference" between human beings is at the root of many of our miseries.

Here the student writes that she had been in Henrietta's shoes, "for a while, in her childhood." And she is trying to address us from the inside, so to speak, of the role of a misunderstood and rejected child. The incident she describes is just an illustration, as she points out, of a tendency among us all.

THE UNSUSPECTED TYRANNY

"Yes, I certainly have got a good nurse for the children now," said the plump hostess in a satisfied tone, as her small daughter left the room. "Just see how promptly Dorothea obeys! No fussing at all; she just gets right up and goes when Sarah calls. And it's always just like that. She used to be a nervous cranky child, too."

The visitor looked dubious. "The child seems pretty nervous to me now," she hazarded. "I never noticed that she stammered before. She didn't last summer, did she?"

The hostess looked a little troubled. "Yes, she *has* begun to stammer a little this winter," she admitted. "I don't quite know what to do about it. I suppose she is growing fast. And she has just begun to go to school. Anyhow, I can tell you it is a relief to me that she is so quiet all day long with this nurse. It makes all the difference, doesn't it, not to have a little hooligan in the house? Do you remember the times we used to have with her last summer?"

Being shy, the visitor made polite noises of assent, but she felt conscience-stricken as she did so. Little Dorothea, with black circles under her eyes, stammering at every other word, starting when the door opened suddenly, was not at all like the gay talkative child—"cranky" but charming—whom she had known the year before. "She positively looks frightened!" thought the visitor.

"Could it be possible that the nurse punishes the children?" she suggested.

"Oh no, my dear!" her hostess rebuked her firmly. "The children would tell me at once if anything like that happened. They know quite well that their nurses are not allowed to punish them without my knowledge. No, it is just that Sarah is firm, and the children know that they have to obey. Won't you have some more tea?"

One—two—three. Dorothea is counting the strokes of the big clock in the hall. Three o'clock is a long while before morning. What was that noise? Is there anyone in the room? Dorothea sits up in bed, her heart pounding. What is that white thing at the window? Is it one of the Ku Klux Klan Sarah talks about, the Terrible People who come in the night to get bad children? No, this time it is only the white curtain waving.

Sarah is snoring in the next bed, but even if Sarah were awake she wouldn't help. The Terrible People are friends of Sarah's—Sarah says so. And she says that everybody is scared of the Ku Klux Klan, even Mother, even Father, even the President of the United States and all the government. They are all so scared that they have to pretend they never heard of the Klan at all. "If you ask your mother about them," says Sarah, "she'll laugh and say it's all foolishness—that's just what she'll say. And it'll be because she's scared they'll come and get *her* in the night if she warns anyone against them."

One day Dorothea did ask her mother. "Are there people dressed all in white who are so bad that everybody is afraid of them?" she asked.

Her mother laughed a comfortable laugh. "Why no, of course not!" she said. "What foolishness have you got into your head now? You certainly have got the wildest imagination, chickie!"

Dorothea stared in silent horror. Her mother did

laugh and say it was "foolishness." So of course Sarah is right. There are such people, and Mother and Father don't dare say so. That's why they laugh. There is no help, anywhere.

What is *that* noise? Step, step, step, out in the hall? Dorothea cannot bear it any longer. She slips out of bed and opens the door. The hall is empty; downstairs a door is swinging to and fro. In her nightgown Dorothea, shivering with cold and terror, explores the day nursery, the bathroom, the dark corner by the back stairs. No one is there except the cold moon looking in at the window. But They will surely come tonight some time. Sarah said so this evening, when Dorothea started to cry because she did not want to go to bed.

Dorothea slips back into bed to wait for them there. Her feet are icy cold. Out in the hall the clock strikes again, once. How many more half hours before They come?

Days and nights of terror have their results. When the nurse left at last, Dorothea slowly came to realize that the nightmare in which she had been living was unreal, that the "Ku Klux Klan" had no power over her. But Sarah had done her work well. Dorothea, now a grown woman, still stammers painfully. Speech is so difficult for her that she is almost entirely cut off from communication with her fellows.

Such hours of devastating terror are fortunately rare in the experience of many children. But every child feels terror at one time or another. For every child is conditioned to a feeling of separation, of "otherness," of difference, whether by a nurse who crudely compels obedience by inculcating fear, or an acquaintance who enjoys frightening the child with gruesome tales, or an overbearing schoolteacher, or a mother who "corrects" the child with physical assault, or one who covers misunderstanding and aggressiveness with an external show of sweetness.

The student could tell us of the terror experienced by this child, for she had known the terror; she had been the child. But she does not realize that her mother and her nurse had also once been children who, although perhaps more subtly, were terrified by the adults about them. The author seems unaware too that threats and terror prevail in the adult world as well as in the lives of children. She does not appreciate that the situation is worldwide. For the universality of the condition was only gradually being recognized in the group investigations at the time the vignette was written.

In the following story, the same student, who had been brought up under rather unusual conditions, again describes her own childhood. She was the daughter of a wealthy family. Her home was a place of continual excitement, always crowded with guests and relatives. In contrast to the small, shy youngster, her father was a large, loud-voiced, self-confident and overactive politician who was much in the public eye. Against this hectic background stands out the figure of a harassed mother endeavoring to meet her varied problems. She had the type of personality that was devastating to the sensitive child—incessant energy combined with extreme gentleness. So that the little girl was quite overborne by her mother's "thoughtfulness." For a "gentle" mother can be as far removed from her child as one who inculcates fear.

"CHRONICAL INDIGESTION"

All the children except one had run shouting out of the schoolroom door and were throwing snowballs in the yard. The one remaining child sidled up to the visitor

and stood looking at her solemnly. The visitor returned
the scrutiny with interest, for this tiny child with the
listless, pale face and frail body had looked singularly out
of place in the rollicking group of seven-year-olds which
had filled the open-air schoolroom a moment ago.

"Aren't you going out to play?" asked the visitor at
last.

"No, ma'am," answered the child. "I can't go out
when it's cold. I'm not strong."

"But it makes people strong to play out-of-doors,"
urged the visitor.

"My mother doesn't want me to. I'm always sick. I
have 'chronical indigestion,'" announced the child, with
a little air of pride, "and my mother has to be very
careful of me."

"Well, but exercise is good for indigestion," repeated
the visitor, a little faintly.

"Oh no, ma'am, not *chronical* indigestion," the child
remonstrated. "Not the kind I have. Last year I couldn't
walk at all! I was so weak I had to be pushed in a wheel-
chair all the time. And I don't eat hardly *anything*.
Until I was five years old I didn't eat anything *at all*
except milk out of a bottle—"

"Nothing but milk out of a bottle until you were five
years old!" interrupted the visitor, rather startled. "I
don't wonder you have indigestion."

"Yes, ma'am!" assented the child almost with enthusiasm. "Everybody says my mother is a very wonderful
woman, the way she brought me up when I was so sick
and all. All the ladies say they don't see how she did it."

The visitor was silent, staring at the child's queer
pallor, bloated stomach, and tiny skinny hands, while
the gentle little voice went on enumerating a long list

of the articles of diet which did or did not "agree" with her. We have all been bored with similar dietaries from certain elderly members of our acquaintance whom we may call "hypochondriac." But when a child of seven is so enamored of her "symptoms" that she will talk of nothing else it makes us more uncomfortable than does mere boredom. "How did she get that way?" the visitor asked herself. And suddenly the visitor realized that it was no more surprising that this child should have memorized a list of foods she might or might not eat than that other children should memorize Mother Goose songs to sing to "company."

There flashed into her mind an imaginary picture of the child's mother surrounded by various admiring "ladies," discoursing on the diet question and the many difficulties which she had encountered in bringing up a child who would drink nothing but milk out of a bottle. By the mother's side is sitting a silent, attentive baby of three. The small girl does not quite know what she has done that is so creditable, but she feels—of course without definitely analyzing it—that the chorus of "My," and "You don't say!" and "Just look how thin the poor child looks!" is pleasing to her mother and that somehow it is up to her to go on being "delicate" and the center of attention. There are drawbacks—she doesn't like a wheel-chair when all the children in the park are on kiddie cars, and she is quite nauseated by the "tonic" which is given her so frequently. But as she hears, times without number, the record of her extraordinary aptitude for illness—to the accompaniment of admiration and petting—what can a lone baby do, who has never once felt the joy of vigorous play, but acquiesce in what is expected of her, and continue to be the living embodiment of her mother's chronicle of indigestion?

In the next sketch, the little boy is the same student in disguise. The beautiful sister she mentions was admired by everyone, and therefore the occasion of many a heartache for the unhappy author of this story.

THE BOY WHO HATED MUSIC

Miss Brandon looked with perplexity at the small boy in front of her. He was such a difficult youngster. When he first came he had spent morning after morning in kindergarten sitting silent and inactive, casting furtive sidelong glances of distrust at the teachers and the children. Lately he had begun to do some handwork and to join in the conversation now and then, but never, in the two months since the opening of school, had he taken any part in the rhythmic games or marching. Now, as usual, he was sitting glued to his chair, with his eyes fixed on the ground, shaking his head when one of the young teachers invited him to join the other children who were standing in line waiting to march.

"No use," whispered the young teacher, "He *is* so obstinate. And he hates music."

And yet Miss Brandon had a feeling that something more than mere obstinacy lay back of his resistance. And as for his "hating music," had she not seen him, the day before, swaying his whole body in time to the children's singing? Had she not been struck by the lilt and swing with which he recited the kindergarten rhymes? Surely it was not lack of rhythmic feeling which was holding him back.

Knowing his shyness, she beckoned him quietly into the cloakroom. He followed her readily.

"Harry, you know I like you, don't you?" she began.

"Yes," he replied.

"Well, I'm not going to *make* you do anything you

don't want to do," she went on. "If you really don't want to march you don't have to. But in that case when you go home today I'm afraid you had better tell your mother not to send you back to school any more, because I can't have a little boy in my class who is not willing to help me. If you like school and want to stay, when we go back in the other room we can march together. I'll walk right beside you, and we can hold each other's hands. But if you would rather leave school it will be perfectly all right. You can choose which you would rather do."

Harry considered for a long moment. In the next room the children's feet thumped cheerfully to a gay tune. "I'll march," he announced at last.

Miss Brandon could tell by the clutch of his fingers on hers that his first march was a struggle. Once he bumped against a chair throwing himself out of step for a moment, and a look of terror came into his face, but when she reassured him he regained courage and went on. Toward the end he evidently began to enjoy himself and, before many days were over, at the first sound of the piano he was alert and enthusiastic. What had been back of his previous reluctance?

If Miss Brandon had been present at his first introduction to the difficulties of marching, she would have understood. Once when Harry was about three, an energetic young lady visitor undertook to instruct his older sister in the mysteries of rhythmic dancing. The little girl was skipping and marching to Mother Goose melodies, while Harry stood watching, his eyes round with wonder. Finally the young lady noticed him. It always took any visitor some time to notice Harry when his sister was there.

"Don't you want to skip too?" inquired the young lady casually.

Harry's face lighted up. He had no idea that he could

possibly be included in this fascinating experience. He took the young lady's hand and that misguided young person, disregarding his tender years and his evident clumsiness, started to skip down the room. At the second step Harry fell sprawling. There burst forth a howl far surpassing the measure of his physical hurt. He wept bitterly for many minutes. And during the remainder of the young lady's visit he would never try to dance again. He would watch his sister with absorbed interest; he would listen to the Victrola for half an hour at a time; but he had made up his mind that this beautiful dream of motion was not for him. It was only for his "graceful" sister.

Perhaps we do not realize how often some such experience lies behind the "unaccountable," "annoying" behavior of both children and adults. Something has hurt us all. Something has killed our spontaneity. The standard of comparison always about us—"this one is good, that one is bad"—has made us self-conscious and miserable. We adults have become accustomed to blocking most of our interest for fear we might not "do well." And when we see an unhappy, self-conscious child we do not want to look for the clue to his unhappiness. If we found it, it might involve an indictment of our whole system of thought. We do not see that we are telling the child every day and every hour that he must live up to certain specifications. He must be as good as Johnny and a great deal better than Tommy. Even the more discerning among us can only offer the child the choice of conforming to the system or of "leaving school."

This handful of stories depicts universal emotional patterns, not the reactions of one Henrietta, not the behavior of a special mother or a special child. But of deepest significance for the problem of child-rearing is the universal mood that is subtly instilled, the mood that "knows" it is "right" and that points to one person as "good" and acceptable, and to the other as "bad" and unwelcome. This mood, with its categorical divisioning, is thoroughly artificial and undependable. It motivates the hardhearted landlord who knows he is "right" and has no qualms when he evicts his poverty-stricken tenants; or the canny industrialist who hires contract labor at illegal wages; or the nation which threatens the peace of the world for the sake of its own prestige. But the identical mood motivates landlord, industralist, or nation when they make generous and high-minded gestures, as they are quite capable of doing. Being ulterior, the mood in both these alternative reactions is bound to issue in inconsistent behavior.

The preceding pieces have presented various aspects of a condition that accounts for much of man's present pain. The following essay paints the picture in its broad social outline. It indicates that, even in 1923, the first intimations of the racial character of the problem had been envisaged by the initiators of group- or phylo-analysis.

THE RECIPROCAL IMAGE

We are all living other people's lives for them; we are all permitting other people to live our lives for us. We pattern our lives solely upon what other people think our lives ought to be; we demand that other people adjust their lives in accordance with the pattern we lay down for them. For thoughts of our own we substitute the opinions of other people; in place of other people's thoughts we impose upon them our own opinions. In this mutual exchange of mental prejudices reflected in our social images of one another lies the real cause of the spiritual inertia among us with its attendant lack of spontaneous productivity in creative interests.

This trick by which we prevail upon people to discard their own initiative in favor of our arbitrary opinions is most pernicious when applied under circumstances that render its victims an especially easy mark for this type of hoodwinking, namely, when applied to the lives of children and of young people.

I do not know any impediment to life that is more insidious than this habit, into which we have unconsciously fallen, of inducing in the minds of young persons a quite automatic sense of dependence upon the preconceived mental patterns or opinions which we have ourselves adopted through an identical social mechanism as it was applied in our own childhood.

I have in mind at the moment a boy of unquestioned talent and originality whose initiative is held completely in leash by the presumptive attitude of personal opinionativeness or so-called "responsibility" expressed toward him by his parents. They wonder why John "doesn't do anything," why he has "no interest in anything," or any sense of obligation to "get down to work." It does not occur to them that it is precisely their wonderment that is John's real impediment, that their autocratic sponsorship toward the condition is the whole occasion of the condition. For, deep within the native organic centers of John's consciousness, John knows with a primordial knowing that to act from within himself is to act of himself, that spontaneous activity is a condition that precludes all motives to action through inducements imposed from without. Inherently he knows that if he is really to meet life on his own, he cannot be prompted to action by a suggestive social imitation that has been transmitted to him from his home environment. John feels the paralysis induced within him by the influence of these mesmeric images that surround him, but in the overpowering magnitude of their social supremacy he is ineffectual to outwit them.

This frustration of effectiveness, of which we are the impotent witnesses in the individual instance of John, is but one superficial symptom of a disorder that is social. We have learned that dissociation occurring within the individual personality is not to be remedied by concentrating upon the particular image, illusion, or substitution that is the mere isolated symptom of a general disorder within the individual. So, within the social personality the isolation and study of one manifest expression of its disorder as represented in the individual do not reach and remedy the essential social disharmony. A social disorder that is systemic can be remedied only through measures directed toward the social system.

CHAPTER V

The Social Neurosis

Phylobiology is the study of the species man in relation to his social environment. As we saw in Chapter II, it posits coordinated interrelational function as the essential basis of healthy behavior—a functional coordination analogous to that existing between the right and the left hand of the individual. These investigations show that this primary functional unity has been set aside and that we now attempt to make contact with our fellow men through the restrictive part-reactions of the symbolic segment. The sketches we have just been reading describe some developmental aspects of this substitutive process. They indicate how the children of each generation are led to repress their total organismic feeling and subject themselves to the authority of an affective mental symbol "right" as interpreted by their parents. The social consequences of the disruption of man's organismic feeling and the substitution of self-centered, partitive affects are severe and widespread. Disorder and conflict reign supreme throughout the sphere of our interrelational behavior, and we live in the midst of a *social neurosis.*

There are two universal characteristics of the social neurosis.

First, a concentration on the part or item to the exclusion of the whole; and second, a moral or right-wrong evaluation of human behavior. The discerning reader may have noted many evidences of these two tendencies in the stories written during the early years of group analysis. For while it is repeatedly *said* in these stories that "we all react in the same neurotic manner," there is nevertheless the presence of a *mood* that itemizes and isolates. The zest and dramatic interest is reserved for that part of the narrative in which the finger is pointed at an isolated instance of disordered behavior or at the reactions of one special individual. The compulsion of the social neurosis did not permit the students to feel the phylic nature of the disorder. Likewise, the writers quite often reveal evidences of a moral attitude in respect to the material they are attempting to observe. It is apparent that they are thinking of disordered behavior as delinquent rather than pathological. Their attitude is not objective; it still remains to a considerable extent on the subjective, affective level. The inference is that, given a little thought, a few admonitions, and a good program of reform, all will be well. As students, even while analyzing the symptoms of the social neurosis, we often demonstrated the very disordered feeling we were supposedly observing. In holding up the mirror to normality, we too often forgot to turn it on ourselves.

The moral attitude that criticizes this or that person as being in the "wrong" is the inevitable fruit of those nursery admonitions we have seen to be part and parcel of the conditioning of the infant generation. As the nursery is a universal institution, so the neurosis which it breeds is a universal condition. We live and move in this neurosis which we call normal life and do not for a moment recognize that every conversation in which we take part, every opinion we form, every liking or disliking that motivates our relations with other people is, from the standpoint of primary, organismic feeling, twisted and askew.

There is no lack of evidence that man realizes his plight, at least intellectually. Historians and economists offer theories aplenty to account for such phenomena as inequality of opportunity, crime, and war. Artists and novelists have depicted the strange and monstrous inconsistencies of human behavior. Systems of religion and philosophy are built upon the realization that the mass of men live "lives of quiet desperation." Prophets and poets have sung the epic tragedy of man. But the researches with which this book is concerned set resolutely aside all opinions and beliefs based on a moralistic interpretation of behavior. As Dr. Burrow makes plain in *The Neurosis of Man*, the phylobiological investigation is an attempt to reach a level of understanding and communication that is more fundamental. It abrogates personal opinions and beliefs, and is concerned with reactions directly observable within and by the observers themselves. In this procedure there was no precedent to guide the course of the research. There was simply the attempt at direct observation of inter-relational behavior from the standpoint of its biological and phylic significance.

At the time of the publication of *Mental Health*, Dr. Burrow's investigations had not yet established a fundamental basis of observation and communication. That basis was arrived at only with the perfecting of a technique for observing and correlating internal patterns of tension. But the challenge of various aspects of so-called normal human interrelations as they occurred in the group was incessant, so that many of the sketches betoken at least an intellectual appreciation of a behavioral dissociation in which all the students shared.

The inner story of Mark Twain's life is the magnified or glorified story of each of us. If a man wishes to know who he is and what he is doing, let him read *The Ordeal of Mark Twain* by Van Wyck Brooks. Undoubtedly nearly everyone on reading this book will be surprised to find that Mark Twain ever knew an ordeal, that life was at any time for him other than a glad carefree party. But for every humorous book he wrote there was a serious one, for every literary success there was an artistic failure, for every elation a depression, for every light a shadow.

The Mark Twain we know publicly was chiefly the Mark Twain in his happy phase; he capitalized, one might say, his elation and made his fortune from it. But elation, we know, is not progressive; it is not creative, it is desperate action without reflection; it is not life and it is not art, and Samuel Clemens as revealed in his boyhood and young manhood must have been inherently of the artist type.

Apparently, in the small western town in which Clemens was born, it was impossible to be anything out of the average; it was an intolerable breach of the frontier code for anyone to be different from his fellows. It marked him out as being pretentious in a situation where everyone made a show of equality. So a creative artist, and especially a creative poet or writer could not have existed there except as a creature apart. And we know from Clemens' own remark that he could not have stood the mental isolation this would have entailed. Says he, "Perhaps there is something that man loves more than he does peace—the approval of his neighbors and the public. And perhaps there is something which he dreads more than he dreads pain—the disapproval of his neighbors and the public." At the same time, to get on was one of the first commandments of Hannibal, Missouri and all of America at that time, and being unpopular is not thought to be the surest way to get on.

But there was one channel in which a man could show his ability and his cleverness, his penetration and his creative imagination. This was to be a humorist. It is the characteristic of frontier humor that it says its serious unorthodox or even tragic thoughts under cover of a smile. And American humor and this type of humor are identical.

And why is it that Mark Twain was so popular? It is because we like in people what we see of ourselves in them, because Mark Twain is the embodiment of what we ourselves are, he says what we would like to say and sometimes do say. He has been called the typical American. He is in reality the typical human. He is ourselves.

Brooks feels in the early part of his book that Mark Twain, through repression chiefly on the part of his mother, chose an oblique expression for his creative impulses, namely, an art inferior to his ability, and suffered his depressions and obsessions and rages as an inevitable result of a thwarted nature. Later Brooks says, "He is the symbol of the creative life in a country where 'by the goodness of God, we have those three unspeakably precious things: freedom of speech, freedom of conscience, and the prudence never to practice either.' "

This expresses more our own feeling. To us the process seemed to begin very early in Clemens' life as it does with all of us; his mother had no more to do with it than all the other citizens of Hannibal and America, too, for that matter. At infancy he was inducted into the code of his times, the mutual agreement born of fear which everyone then held, whose prime requisite was that everyone give up his independence of thought and whose promised reward in exchange was the illusion of material success. And all his life he fretted at this code but remained within its confines. But Mark Twain is not alone in this, it is the experience of everyone, as each of us who looks back to his childhood can confirm.

A national idol, a national spokesman, can say only what his contemporaries say; the prophet is he who utters what his contemporaries think and do not often say; the artist expresses what his contemporaries think but do not dare admit to themselves. True artists are very rare and not infrequently die young.

And so we can see why Mark Twain could survive only by virtue of being like the crowd. One person can not think his way out alone, he dies from the loneliness of the attempt and from popular disapproval. Thinking is really a cooperative matter. Only a group of people thus can think a way out for the race, but a group of people can do so.

The student who wrote the preceding review emphasizes the common aspect of human life that forces every human being into the same ordeal of frustration that Van Wyck Brooks presents as an experience peculiar to Mark Twain. This student was responding to the stimulus of constant emphasis in the group sessions upon the generic nature of human reactions, and the need of a common, group approach to the problem of interpersonal relations. But his was as yet an intellectual appreciation only. It did not touch his feeling, which remained obdurately apart. When, in the course of group analysis, we as students were challenged in our authoritarian "rightness," we were "mad enough to bite." There was no sense of functional unity among us. Each was out to protect to the death his personal distinction. The contrast between the reiterated appeal in our stories for a group approach to human behavior and the complete lack of group feeling in day-by-day living furnished corroborative evidence of the presence among us of a social neurosis that forced us into this behavioral inconsistency.

There is pain, deep, organic pain, attendant upon such disunity. But it would seem that our habitual submission to the image we absorbed in the nursery—the image of our own prestige—compels us to ignore the pain for the sake of preserving that precious image at all costs. The next essay is concerned with this phase of our social neurosis.

THE HIGH PRICE OF PAIN

We are accustomed to think of pain as an unwarranted infliction upon us of forces or conditions that operate wholly apart from ourselves. Only under the stimulus of anger, competition or jealousy—a circumstance in which we are afforded the obvious pleasure of inflicting pain upon others—do we recognize pain as a function of our own will. But the pain which we ourselves experience we have utterly failed as yet to regard as in any sense allied with our own volition. Until now we have not recognized our personal pain as involving in any way our own personal advantage.

We are all familiar with the role which the offering of sacrifice occupied in ancient and in medieval times. This element of self-denial preserves its place amid many of our present-day observances. Our Lenten offerings are examples of sacrifice prompted by this same underlying motive of pain. Yet all these curtailments of our immediate desires have as their aim the central purpose of atonement, or an adjustment to the end of future satisfaction. Viewed impartially, analytically, it has to be admitted that such discomforts and incommodities stand to us in the light of a profitable exchange. They are the price we pay here for larger benefits hereafter. In this spirit what we give up in this world is merely a return for promises of a larger satisfaction in the world to come.

But we need not have recourse to the time-honored practices of asceticism and self-denial in illustration of the profits of pain. The pain and denial of life we voluntarily undergo in the quite ordinary routine of our habitual days exemplify this identical mechanism. The long, tedious hours we compel ourselves to spend in close, unbeautiful offices, the irksome strictures we impose upon ourselves as members of a particular political system or social set, the discomforts and even illness we constantly incur through excesses of eating—these and countless other self-inflictions are no less the price we pay for our satisfactions in the moment at hand.

The pain of long office hours is recompensed with wealth, the strictures of the social code with "position," while in the ever-renewed round of pleasant-tasting foods we are amply requited for the disorders due to our dietary indiscretions. Perhaps of all the tolls we exact of ourselves in obedience to the despotic mastery of pain, by far the heaviest consists in the wranglings into which from hour to hour we are obsessively led in our restless effort to substantiate our own opinions as from time to time they appear menaced by the opinions of other people. The pain of proving ourselves "right" is second only to the pain of finding ourselves wrong. Yet in our ingrained mental habituations how willingly we concede the price of such feverish perturbations of spirit for the satisfaction of securing to our egotism its private advantage. And so it would seem that pain is not so much a visitation upon us as a bargain we make with it in the interest of returns which, as we believe, will redound ultimately to our greater good.

Those who have entered into the deeper recesses of diseased mental states cannot but mark this same element of commerce with pain or fail to note that the factor of bargain and self-interest is the essential occasion for the psychic pain entailed. The difference is that in the normal pain incurred in the interest of normal profits, the market fluctuations, so to speak, are less extreme. The variations in its rise and fall are not so marked, nor has one staked his all upon its uncertain issues. But in the pathological subject his enterprises entail far more serious alternatives, and not seldom he is involved to the extent of all his spiritual holdings. Under such circumstances it is easily seen why at one period he finds himself lifted to the seventh heaven of exhilaration and at another he is cast down to the lowermost depths of self-doubt and despondency.

Man, as has been said, is not without some realization of his insecurity, his loneliness, and his need. But the power of the social neurosis is such that many see in the poignant tragedy of human life merely an opportunity to further their own advantage.

COMMERCIAL PANACEAS

In *The American Mercury* for March 1924 there is reprinted in the department of "Clinical Notes," with the

characteristically Menckenesque subheading "Studies in
Boobology," a series of advertisements which without
question have a deep interest for readers of *Mental Health*.
As originally issued, these advertisements in part claim
through their titles to come from institutions of learning.
Of these, one is frankly a publishing house. It claims,
however, for its publications—the work of Col. Robert G.
Ingersoll—that through the mere reading of them, no
position will be either "socially or commercially" beyond
the grasp of the reader. The remainder offer as tempting
bait to prospective nibblers anything and everything from
the "confidence, love, obedience and respect of your
child" to "power of creative thought," from ability to
"overcome illness and poverty" to a method of staying
young by keeping the "spine a half-inch longer than it
ordinarily would measure."

The tone of these advertisements leaves no doubt that
they represent purely commercial enterprises—eight of
them located in five States of the Union from Massa-
chusetts to Minnesota. At least two, not including the
publishing house—and probably all—offer their cure-all
for character defects by means of correspondence courses.

There is small cause to waste energy deploring the
spirit of cupidity that has inspired the development of
these organizations. Appalling, however, is the thought
of the suffering and need that support the human para-
sites who at distant desks pretend to respond by means
of a postage stamp to the poignant demand for the most
delicate and subtle of all personal contacts.

From the point of view of *Mental Health* these "in-
stitutes" and "schools" are to be regarded not as a helpful
development, but rather as the ready source of an increase
in the very difficulties for which they offer a panacea.
Placing a premium on "success," on "doubling, trebling

or even quadrupling your salary," on the development of an ability to "persuade people to do what you want them to do," they establish a ready-made standard of life to which men and women will try to adapt themselves, inevitably inviting failure on the part of many. With a keen business instinct these promoters undertake to exploit the human weakness which in large part has resulted from the very thing they represent. Sensing a widespread need they offer in the form of medicine the concentrated essence, so to speak, of that very spirit of competition which has already proved a poison to the victims they pretend to be able to cure. There is involved the sort of cruelty that whips a horse, fallen through weakness, to make him try to draw the load again. Humane members of society have organized to protect unfortunate animals from human cruelty. Is there any protection for prospective human victims?

Apparently there is no attitude too pitiless, no subterfuge too callous to be adopted by the individual in pursuit of his own self-advantage. Perhaps the following piece will give an intimation of the disordered mood out of which our behavior springs.

FALSE CLAIMS

I am in the throes of a tantrum. I do not know that this is so, any more than while I dream I know that I am dreaming. For while I dream I am sure that I am awake, and my tantrum can last only so long as I am convinced that it is not a tantrum. And so I continue to lie gripped by the dream that is my tantrum even while I appear to be walking among men, and my dream becomes a horrible nightmare.

I am indulging in an orgy of self-pity. My self-pity

is as a blurred glass through which I look at the world about me, and I refuse to see that the glass is not clear. In my delusion I resort to tricks so that I can pose in the role I have selected, so that I can give the appearance of having been hurt by others. Then I can put the blame on them and perhaps secure the support I am looking for in the indulgence of my pity for myself.

With my blurred vision I see others attacking the province that I claim for myself—my rights, my privileges, my opportunities—anything, everything I see slipping away from me, and I lie helpless, unable to do anything but utter meaningless complaints. If I arouse myself from my dream I shall know that what I am claiming does not belong to me. For that which is really mine none can take from me, and that to which I must lay claim can in no sense be really mine.

In my delusion I flatter myself that I do not want that which is not mine, and I struggle against awakening to know that this is not true. I refuse to acknowledge— most of all to myself—that all my life I have laid claim to that which did not belong to me. If it were offered to me by others, I encouraged their offers. If there were those who made claim against me for that which I held as my own, I looked upon them scornfully and labeled their claims as false.

Always my thought revolves dizzily about situations with but a single theme, and that theme is concern for myself and that which I consider mine—my ability, my accomplishments, my reputation. And thus I continue to keep my hand raised against every man, while in my dream I see only their hands raised against me.

What is the point of all this self-concern? What does

it mean? Where can it lead? If I arouse myself from my dream I shall know that it leads nowhere—it can lead nowhere except to such false claims as I am making. There can be no such thing as a claim for that which really belongs to me.

Even the tantrum, the self-pity, the false claims are not mine, for you are indulging in them also, and you and you. If you tell me that this is not true, that is only your false claim. On all sides I am supported and encouraged, for in a world in which false claims are unknown, I cannot make false claims.

According to phylobiology, this "I" that occupies the center of the stage for each of us is the heart of man's neurosis. It is rooted and grounded in affect, in false feeling, and it awakens affect or false feeling in the people with whom we associate throughout the day. But each of them also has his secret cinema in which he is the star. Is it any wonder, then, that our family life, our industrial relations, our political parleys are marked by discord and confusion? As this is written, a great industrial strike is in progress. President Truman has tried to avert it by appointing a fact-finding board. Man is forever setting up fact-finding boards and assemblies and judiciary courts in his effort to arrive at a dispassionate and objective solution of fundamental human problems concerning the relation of the individual to society. But always the image of the "I" interposes between the organism's primary function and the situation to be observed. No matter how calm and fair is the external aspect of these boards, they are composed of men and women each of whom has been nurtured in the profound sense of his separate authority apart from the group. There is always a point at which the individual ceases to see a fact objectively and looks at it through a mist of affect. But, however widespread its occurrence, such a reaction indicates behavioral imbalance and neurosis.

Although this dark picture of a dissociated species was constantly manifested in the group sessions, the experimenters continued undaunted in their social analysis. They were not deterred in their effort to discover an underlying cause that could be verified and would at the same time be broad enough to account for the racial scope of the disorder.

IS INSANITY A SOCIAL RESPONSIBILITY?

Many people think that insanity is a condition quite apart from the ordinary impressions and activities that enter into the daily living of each of us. We do not think of insanity as a condition having to do with a false way of looking at the facts of life as they are presented from moment to moment in the casual circumstances of our habitual days. We hesitate to recognize that it is the habit of mind whereby we infer the significance of the facts before us not in the light of what they are but in the light of what we would like them to be. In brief, insanity is our preference for viewing life not as it is, but as we would have it. It is to surrender thought to the caprice of emotion.

The point is, though, that as such tendencies are general, they are inseparable from our social habituations and beliefs. Hence insane tendencies of adaptation are not to be remedied except as they are regarded from the point of view of their social significance. This means that in dealing with the phenomena of mental disorders our attack must be forthright and unflinching. Up to the present time we have hesitated to challenge our accustomed thought. We have slipped too easily into the attitude of mind that merely palliates and condones.

This is to make light of insanity. This is to avoid recognizing its true implications. To attempt to palliate the seriousness of insanity by making light of it is as shortsighted as it is sentimental. The condition is a truly serious one. The somberness of the situation cannot be exaggerated. On the other hand, our attitude would be equally restricted and sentimental if we permitted the gloom that rests upon the features of insanity to darken our outlook upon it.

Because the external picture offers so painful and forbidding an aspect, it does not mean that the actuality underlying disordered states of mind is inaccessible to the remedial measures of a proper scientific approach. Although the symptoms presented upon the surface are serious and distressing, nevertheless the condition represented by them belongs for the most part within the domain of the disorders that are correctible.

The success of the surgeon does not consist in cheerfully dismissing the alarming character of his patient's symptoms. He does not attempt to mitigate the terrible dangers of malignant tumor with the evasive unconcern of an easy-going optimism. On the contrary the success of the surgeon lies in fearlessly facing the seriousness of the condition before him and resolutely approaching it through decisive recourse to the knife.

In the realm of surgery there are comparatively few derangements of the physical organism which if taken in hand in their early stages may not be approached with entire confidence of recovery. Likewise in the realm of psychiatry there is no functional impairment of the mental processes which, if recognized at its onset or in its early course, may not be approached with equal assurance of complete readjustment. To the physician of physical ailments no manifestation seems hopeless where through timely intervention the conditions permit its being regarded scientifically; so too, wherever through timely conditions mental disorders may be treated scientifically, analytically, no situation (barring structural change due to some noxious or infectious process) is too formidable to the physician who has to deal with the disorders of the mind.

The physician, however, fails to compass the disorders of the mind who does not recognize the broad social involvement of these disharmonies. He cannot truly correct these discrepancies of emotion, these distortions of mental outlook, as long as he regards them as exceptional and isolated processes. It is only as he comes to view them as exaggerations of habitual tendencies common to us all that he may cope understandingly with the pathology of disordered mental states.

There is a forecast here of the later findings of the phylobiological laboratory. These revealed that the biased image of the "I," which is the center of our emotional life, is not an individual phenomenon. It is a vast system of interlocking affects upon which all our political, educational, and domestic institutions are based.

CHAPTER VI

The Social Image

When Jane Eyre discovers at the steps of the altar, where she is to marry Edward Rochester, that he already has a wife, she announces her determination to part from him forever. In answer to his plea that no one will care what she does, since she has no family and no friends, she says:

> "*I* will care. . . . I will keep the law given by God and man. . . . I will hold to the principles received by me when I was sane and not mad—as I am now. . . . Preconceived opinions, foregone determinations are all I have at this hour to stand by; there I plant my foot."

The hearts of many readers swell with admiration of Jane's lofty spirit, and they long to emulate her dauntless fortitude. From a scientific outlook in respect to behavior, however, she is as completely unbalanced when she leaves her lover as she is when in the grip of her passion for him.

What is the nature of these principles, these preconceived opinions by which Jane takes her stand with such indomitable courage? For one thing, they are not consistent and immutable throughout mankind. They cluster about the ideal of marriage as it existed in Victorian England. If Jane and Rochester had been Hindus or Mohammedans, there would have been no occasion for heroics. For another thing, Jane's "principles" are purely mental concepts swaying her toward a type of behavior she had been trained to think is right. But her feelings surge in the opposite direction and she becomes immersed in a profound internal conflict.

Jane Eyre was the product of that childhood conditioning which, as we have seen, interposes a symbol of "the right" between the organism and its direct response to the environment. In the course of the child's conditioning, the symbol of "right" becomes personified in the image of the mother— not only his biological mother but also his teachers, all the molders of his mind. The self-interested feelings that form the core of his spurious personality cluster about the illusion of a tremendous power that is infinitely strong and infinitely wise. Such illusions due to affect become deeply ingrained in the child and are fully corroborated by the community. In phylo-biology an affect-image cherished by the community had been termed a "social image."

The social image of the mother, and of the father, too, is closely intertwined with the child's image of the "I," because to the child it means security, authority, the constant cor-roboration of his sense of himself as a special being—a being apart from the general run of men. So that Jane Eyre's ex-clamation, "Preconceived opinions, foregone determinations are all I have at this hour to stand by; there I plant my foot," is in reality an ardent appeal to the image of the parent. For all its grandiloquent tone, it expresses a retrogression to the nursery. But because the image of the mother is a social image before which we all bend the knee, this passage has been one of the most cherished in English literature.

Social images, stemming as they do from the image of the parent or the image of the "I," are clusters of affect and prejudice adhering to certain mental concepts of right behavior. They differ in various human groups. It is "right" to conform to our moral code, so we have built up the social image of the law. It is "right" to be kind, so we have established the social image of courtesy, a system of rules for *appearing* kind. Marital devotion is "right," so husbands and wives enact devotion, often at the cost of crippling their own potentialities. It is "right" to fight for one's country. "My country, right or wrong" is better than any other country. So we have the grand social image of nationalism, with its inescapable sequel, war. It is not too much to say that our social images may yet be the death of us.

Innumerable social images have fashioned the life of man in the past and still fashion it today. Those which have had their day and become obsolete we tend to regard with indifference or disdain—the divine right of kings, slavery, the superiority of the nobility, the literal inspiration of the Bible. We watch people in other countries behaving in ways that seem to us fantastic. But, judged by the standard of a biological norm, their behavior is not more fantastic than our own.

The reader must be reminded that we are here describing the symptomatology of a dissociation that, according to phylobiology, seriously distorts the life of individual and community. While this description may seem dreary reading to the layman, familiarity with all the morbid and unpleasant characteristics of a disease, bacterial or behavioral, is essential if one hopes successfully to diagnose it and bring it under control. As we know, the individual organism of every sick patient carries within it an inherent capacity for health. Likewise the organism of man as a species is endowed with an infinite power to achieve behavioral coordination and balance. How else

can we explain the continued survival of the species in spite
of the antagonism and conflict among its elements? Phylobiology is interested solely in cultivating this biological verity
that lies at the heart of life. It is not concerned with disrupt-
ing the institutions that now hold communities together, but
rather with activating the organism's inclusive continuity of
feeling, for which these institutions are merely the inadequate
substitutes. Perhaps the following sketch will afford the reader
an insight into the power of a social image to sunder integrity
of feeling and transform it into mere charade.

THE WORLD AND HIS WIFE

"I wouldn't want anybody to hear me say it, but if it
were not that I am the wife of Dr. Maitland, I'd love nothing better than to go on the stage as a professional
dancer." "It seems to me," I said, "that if as the wife of
Dr. Maitland you are inhibited in the expression of your
natural interests you are just in so far not his wife. You
are simply pretending to be—merely *acting a role* like so
many other people calling themselves married."

Only a moment before, this recalcitrant young wife
had been offering me the benefits of her chastening
counsel on the score that I "never said what I really
thought." So here was my opportunity and I was off, glad
to find myself running with so loose a neck having once
dared to free myself from the galling girth of my accustomed social harness. I can still see the sparks of anger
and defiance that snapped from the fiery eyes of Mrs.
Maitland into mine. But what mattered it? In my natural
and unhindered flight I was a bird upon the air. Having
found my wings, the world of enforced "proprieties" was
quickly fading into nothingness. I was addressing the
chief performer in a social drama I seemed now to have

left far behind me. And so, nothing daunted, I held my course.

"It is really too bad," I sped on, "and, worse tragedy, it is quite unnecessary." The world had now become but a speck beneath me. "There are today no end of people who, like yourself, are protesting, if not openly at least in secret, how much they would like to be in this or that situation if they did not have to act like the people in some other—how much they would like *to be* such and such, if they did not have to behave *as if* they were something else. But this attempt to reconcile two contending elements in oneself is to compromise both. The truth is you are not Mrs. Maitland. You have gotten into the costume of Mrs. Maitland. You have made yourself up for the part. You have learned the lines appropriate to the role for which accident or circumstance has cast you. Like so many other wives composing the tawdry chorus conventionally ranged opposite their husbands upon the social stage, you are the impersonator of a part. In your heart of hearts you live in music halls where you are acclaimed the foremost *danseuse* of the hour. But in the unreal and artificial part you act in your daily living we find you simulating the devoted wife who, with the mock gaiety that is weary with enforced repetition, eagerly greets her husband's homecoming as he returns each evening from the round of his professional visits."

"Your behavior is intolerable," burst out Mrs. Maitland, unable to contain herself any longer. "I refuse to listen to such insolence. How dare you say that I do not love my husband more than anyone in the world? You would try to separate my husband and me. Your assertions are sheer impertinence."

But, secure in the wider medium of my new-found

freedom, I was soaring too high by this time to be captured in this too familiar net. "You are still acting, still playing the wife," I replied. "You do not really think me impertinent in the least. You are again repeating the lines of 'a good wife.' You would really exult in what I am saying and feel the freedom and gladness of it as deeply as I do if you could once, as I have done, step out of your accustomed imitations of a wife and, having wiped from your face the customary coating of social cosmetic and habitual grimace, you would dare for once to stand forth as the real wife that you are—the wife that your deeper nature and woman's instinct qualify you to be. Far from wishing to separate you from your husband, my only thought is to have you feel how much closer to him you really are than you yourself have ever yet suspected. Do you think I haven't been the actor of a part as well as you? Do you think I haven't myself played the captive wife, enjoying the role I played opposite my husband just as you enjoy the part you play opposite yours? Do you think I would speak to you now as I am speaking to you, feeling not the slightest concern or fear for your habitual dramatics, if I had not recognized in myself and my husband the same artificiality, the same stupid dramatization and pretense which you and your husband and others of our so-called 'set' are forever enacting? You and Albert have, in fact, the very deepest bonds in common with each other, and you would realize that it is these deeper ties that are of real significance to you both, were it not that your respective pretenses toward one another quite bar you from the opportunity of discovering the natural congeniality between you."

Mrs. Maitland was weeping. "I know," I said in response to her sobs, "but your tears are again part of the actress' stage business when she thinks she has not been all that she might be to her devoted husband. Your thought, as attested by your tears, is still only of your personal appearance in the role you have personally essayed to play. What I am speaking to you of, though, is not any sentimental personal frailty either of yours or mine. This foolish drama we men and women are hypnotized into performing day in and day out is too serious and widespread a mental fallacy for us to take in any personal sense, resenting all reference to it at one moment with hot anger and at another with equally cherished tears. Let me tell you something. We two are supposed to have known each other for a long time. But in fact we are the completest strangers to one another. I have never admitted it even to you, but until lately I had always acted as unconscious a part as you are acting now. I had committed to memory the lines set down for me as faithfully as you have committed yours. Only in the last months and quite by accident has it happened that I have been seriously contemplating this situation with a few earnest men and women who, like myself, have been caught up in the silly habits of the social imitation around them, and who are earnestly trying to think through the insincerity of these social tendencies as they are reflected equally within themselves. It is an unwelcome task they have undertaken, this self-investigation of their only too ready mental habituations. It has been no less unwelcome to me. This unconscious habit of acting is very strong in us all. The satisfaction of approval is very intriguing to our entire company of unconscious social players and when, through the long accustomedness of the years we have come to know only acting, to live only in the part we play, we seem to lose all reckoning of the actual world of our throbbing human feeling and sensibilities. We think—all of us—that if for once we should lose our grasp upon the habitual part, the accustomed role, all our props would be removed from under us and we would lack all the essential supports necessary to life. But experience, investigation, actual experiment do not bear us out in this apprehension. In point of fact our human relationships, when we test their truth by the measure of demonstrable evidence, have proved far closer, far more real than we have ever dared to suspect because of this long-standing habit of artificial adaptation and pretense toward one another."

The actress in Mrs. Maitland was no longer weeping. Neither was she ranting now in the effort to display the anger she had been taught is due whenever reality ventures to intrude itself upon her characterization and rudely threatens the illusory scene of her domestic charade. At last Mrs. Maitland began for the first time to recognize chat in me, her lifelong friend, she had found someone who did not stand opposite her, that here at last was no audience for whom she was compelled to act according as her long training in stage-business demanded of her.

"For months," Mrs. Maitland began, "I have felt completely estranged from you. Whenever I have been with you of late I have felt irritated by your presence. I have thought at times that you must surely recognize it but my resentment completely overpowered me. I feel I can tell you this now. I know now that it does not matter to you. I have not understood you in the least. I have only been determined to believe that the fault must somehow be yours. I suppose that there too I was acting again. I suppose I had to believe that the fault was yours else it would have shaken the security of my entire stage-setting.

I realize now that there need no longer be this shadow of misunderstanding between us. I have felt how close should be our confidence toward each other but I have feared it as much as I have wished it. But the spirit in which you have spoken to me today means very much to me. I realize there is much for me to learn about myself —much that I have myself not guessed the existence of. Like everyone else in the hurrying competitive world of today I have taken myself for granted and insisted that others should do so too. There *is* the need of earnest self-inquiry on my part no less than on yours, and perhaps in your companionship I may yet discover a place for myself in a mode of living that is deeper, fuller and more real."

Man has not been wholly unaware of the tragic waste of capacities involved in such situations as that outlined in the foregoing essay. Artists and poets and religious leaders have commented with deep feeling on the apparently hopeless problem of man's subjection to the tyranny of custom. But they have not reckoned with the reflex reaction to social images established in early childhood.

Great satirists like Voltaire, Dickens, and Daumier have recognized the absurd aspects of certain social institutions— the law, the marital relation, organized philanthropy. Their laughter played its part in the relinquishment by the community of many social vagaries. They did not, however, have the faintest inkling of the presence among us of a social neurosis in which they themselves participated. Indeed, Dickens may be credited with a large share in creating one of the outstanding social images of our time, our cult of Christmas. Before his day, Christmas was a mildly pleasant religious festival. Dickens put all the force of his extraordinary love of coziness, of good food and drink, of jolly companionship, of hearth and home into his paeans of praise for Christmas. But the community, too, loves warmth and coziness and meretricious get-togetherness. The community took Dickens and his Christmas to its heart and wove about his picture of good cheer all the fanciful images of love that make up our artificial unities. Though half the population groans under the burdens this image entails, Dickens and the department stores have established it so securely in the community that nothing short of a social revolution could shake it.

Man has lost his sense of oneness with himself and with his fellow human beings. To compensate for this loss, he must project an image of unity and peace. It is not only the religious significance of the child and the mother that makes them dominate the Christmas scene. To all men, religious and non-religious, the picture of mother and child stands for the indissoluble bond uniting human beings. Mother and child are one. But in our present distorted outlook they are only a symbol, only a picture of unity. Our feeling has been divided and we are no longer one. So we must look at a picture of oneness and "do our Christmas shopping."

Our preoccupation with these symbols of reality imparts a fanciful quality to our thinking and feeling, a quality to which we are so completely inured that, meeting reality face to face, our tendency is to escape into fantasy and dream. There is less difference than we commonly realize between the mental processes of the insane and those of "normal" people. The following review comments on two books that emphasize the unbalanced quality of human behavior.

THE EMPEROR OF PORTUGALLIA

Bernard Hart's small but meaty volume, *The Psychology of Insanity*, lays special emphasis upon the fact that "the thought mechanisms of the so-called insane are the same as those which constitute the thoughts of normal people." This view suggests that an understanding of unbalanced mental states may afford an opportunity for an insight into our thought processes generally. The aberrations of the insane offer this opportunity, if for no other reason than that they are more conspicuous, more dramatic than the mental operations of the ordinary man of the street. The latter is overwhelmed by the innate demand upon him to face life in all its reality and, in his effort to escape the strain he blindly finds too great, he just as blindly seizes upon every possible variety of substitute. Objectively paralleling this situation there is the trite illustration of the factory girl who is exhausted in mind and body by her monotonous day, but who in the evening floats upon a cloud of romance in which she identifies herself with her movie heroine. The factory girl is not interested to ferret out the reason why she finds the screened drama so altogether fascinating. No more do you and I in the least suspect the significance of what we are doing in our constant searching for our favorite substitutes for an unwelcome reality. It is in our failure to know that we too are running away from reality that we look upon the antics of the insane as something foreign to ourselves. But the strangeness lies merely in the fact that, when the insane man decides to leave the land of reality, he plans a journey into an undiscovered country, psychologically speaking. He also, like the ordinary man in the street, is overwhelmed by the innate demand upon him to face life in all its reality, and in his effort to escape he creates a new world to suit himself—a world in which the furnishings are merely a distorted form of the things that are really there. But the insane man is conspicuous among his fellow men merely because the products of his distortion are more grotesque than are theirs.

This possibility that one may take a short cut, so to speak, directly out of a situation that is too painful to bear inspired Selma Lagerlöf, the well-known Swedish author, in the weaving of her touchingly beautiful story. Thus, Jan of Ruffluck Croft, an ordinary peasant who would otherwise have lived and died unnoticed, becomes a picturesque hero, an emperor even, of the land of Portugallia. We are introduced to the man of the fields at the moment when the birth of his golden-haired daughter causes his heart to beat with real emotion for the first time in his life. There develops between him and his baby girl a relationship of which we are told, "It was strange about the little girl of Ruffluck and her father! They seemed to be so entirely of one mind that they could read each other's thoughts!" Within this relationship there is the incident of the school contest. The children were about to be fooled by a trick question, and Glory Goldie saved the day by what seemed an uncanny intuition of the answer in her father's mind. In the course of time the struggling peasant family is about to be crushed economically, and in her effort to save the little home the inexperienced girl of sixteen goes to the city. She falls a victim to the forces that are there, and fails to return at the appointed time with the much-needed money. Not only this, but she cannot even write to her dearly beloved father. Rumors of the painful truth gradually filter through to the parents in their hut, waiting for funds and longing for their child. Now is the loving father called on to face a situation which is too painful for him, and out of it he builds a countersituation in which he can be comfortable. His child, who in the eyes of his neighbors has disgraced him, is by him glorified into a monarch. And merely by the fact of being her father, he, simple Jan of Ruffluck Croft, becomes the Emperor of Portugallia to whom all must bend the knee. He being now too grand for menial duties, his wife must take up the burden of supporting the little household. But in spite of her overwhelming trials—or perhaps because of them—her insight is rare. "Jan is not crazy," she says, "but Our Lord has placed a shade before his eyes so he'll not have to see what he couldn't bear seeing. And for that one can only feel thankful."

True, the peasant woman's insight was rare, but it was with comparative ease that she could interpret so complete a barrier to reality as was Jan's. She still failed to realize, as well she might, that in their own inconspicuous fashion she and her neighbors likewise had shades of their own making. Such a disturbing thought would naturally have challenged her stoutest resistance, even as it does yours and mine. In that resistance we prove our kinship with the Emperor of Portugallia, erstwhile Jan of Ruffluck Croft.

The illusory quality of our thinking and the resulting instability of man's behavior form a large element in interrelational problems. We need the kind of forthright approach to such problems that is represented in the following essay.

MIND AND THE MARKET

Our mental wares have their market just as other products of man. Among our different outputs, whether mental or material, some are staple and some show a fluctuating scale of values. In the sphere of man's material uses it is not the staple article but the temporary commodity for which there is the largest demand. Correspondingly in the sphere of his mental products what is most sound is least marketable. For the deeper expressions of man's personality are, in the light of their commercial appraisement, not comparable to his far less significant products.

The outlay which nations make annually in directions of constructive interests is relatively small, while their expenditures in the machineries of destruction and upon the luxurious and ornamental features of their daily living are rated in figures that are overwhelming. (According to statistics quoted in *The Nation* the expenditure in this country during the past year for cosmetics alone amounted to $750,000,000, while according to figures cited in the *Chicago Daily News* the amount expended in the pursuit of actual destruction represented in the four years of the First World War attained the prodigious sum of $186,000,000,000.) Indeed it would seem to be a law that the market demand for any product as for any project varies inversely as its aptness to the needs of the race as a concerted unit. What is of moment to us, however, is the fact that this inverse proportion between value and demand holds equally in the sphere of our mental exchange. This circumstance is significant in its bearing upon our accustomed habits and predilections of mind. For in inculcating a mental and social attitude of dissipation and dispersion these vagrant trends tend to produce incoherence within the social mind and ultimately to breed discord and insanity among us.

The really great contributions of man's genius, those monuments that represent the closer approximations of thought and feeling—of art and of science—create an interest only among the most rare and responsive personalities. This is because of the approximation of such work to what is *real* as contrasted with the more fanciful dissipations of man's habitual attainments. And so in marketing the products of art as of science it is the supply that is least staple that is most widely demanded. Our newspapers and our journals, our religions and our dramas, our popular novels and our sermons tend to play most artfully with the element of fantasy and of belief and with our dream images generally. For this reason they afford the medium that exerts the strongest influence upon men's mental processes.

Man is a dreamer. He delights in the imagery of unreality. It is his recourse to the indolence of habit as contrasted with the stimuli of growth. And so through the instruments of periodical and pulpit, of the theater and the film he has been alert to capitalize his craving for the superstitious, the sensational and the melodramatic. These and other channels bring entertainment to his fantasy but not substance to his needs.

In face of this intriguing orgy of the fantastic furnished by public propaganda and corroborated by the cheaper output of our so-called art as of our so-called science, it is difficult for educators to inculcate the needed stability of thought that preserves man's consciousness against the lures of the illusory and deceptive. It is in the unharnessed dissipations of fantasy with its countless beliefs and make-believes that are begotten those tendencies of the mind that lead finally to disturbed states in the individual and in the social consciousness. In his abstemiousness toward reality man distorts life with pictured fantasy. It is pleasanter to be entertained with the unreal issues of domestic life as portrayed through the sentimental devices of the novel or the stage than to occupy oneself with the real and pressing problem of setting in order one's own mental and spiritual household. But in our varying extremes of mental self-indulgence we are a prey to the subtle encroachments of aberration and insanity, and in this widespread symptom of our social consciousness there is lacking that solidarity of values in the realm of man's thought that insures his course toward earnest concentration and progress.

As we have seen, it is we of the adult generation, with our "prefabricated beliefs" and our neurotic preoccupation with our prejudices, who decoy the younger generation from its spontaneous relation to the environment and to other members of the species. For the instinct of mating we substitute the social image of "being in love." For the instinct toward wholesome activity we substitute the social image of "making a living." For the instinct toward play we substitute the social image of "having a good time." These vicarious pictures of life assume the same authority for the older child that the parental "yes" and "no" held in his nursery.

The youthful generation of man, deprived of a simple give-and-take relation with the environment, deprived of whole living, becomes a prey to dissociation. There is instability at the heart of life. Together with a sense of separation from the other members of the species goes a deep-seated fear, comparable to that of a person who has lost his sense of balance and feels that at any moment he may fall. We turn to the fanciful security of the social image of "right" as to the arms of a mother. We want to do "right" but at the same time there seems to be an irresistible impulse to do "wrong." Who has not seen the devoted mother who has ungovernable fits of irritability with her child, or the clearheaded businessman who loves to bet on the horses, or the far-seeing statesman who delights in "telling off" his associates even though it means the ruin of his plans. The ambivalence of motivation is expressed everywhere in conflict, not only among neurotic but also among so-called normal people as well.

Ambivalence as an outstanding symptom of the social neurosis was not lost sight of in the group-analytic studies of human behavior. The following essay throws light on the artificial dichotomy that governs man's life today.

MENTAL AMBIVALENCE

There are not in life the basic contrasts that we commonly assume. Among the lower animals the distinction between male and female entails no organic breach. There is oppositeness but not opposition. But with the *mental sophistication* connoted under the distinction "man" and "woman" we have come to assume the presence of an artificial opposition between the male and the female organism. The rigid division between the "artist" and the "artisan," between the dreamer of dreams and the doer of deeds, between people who are "noble" and people who are "base" is equally arbitrary.

These artificial distinctions due to our conventional attitudes of mind are answerable for much needless conflict, as gradually with the individual's growing adaptation he finds himself face to face with the demand that he fit himself into the preconceived pattern of an arbitrary social scheme.

With this artificial condition and its edict of enforced repression there often occurs such a one-sided development within the organism that there results the exaggerated reaction we see in such extremes as the "hero" and the "coward." It is interesting to observe, though, that upon analysis one discovers within the repressed sphere of the coward's personality all the factors that constitute the personality of the hero, and that within the repressed sphere of the hero's personality there are disclosed all the elements that constitute the personality of the coward!

Such findings as we owe to our deeper penetration into individual psychology make clearer the superficiality of our normal, social distinctions. They afford us reason to believe that when education has loosed itself of its superficial acceptations we shall find that wherever the human organism is permitted to live its own life, free from the suggestive influences of differentiation, there will be no longer the repressed or unconscious instigation to such exaggerated distortions or overcompensations as now issue in the protective pretenses of the coward or in the masked bravadoes correspondingly characteristic of the life of the hero.

Under the stubborn despotism of the "right-wrong" image, human personality is not what it seems to be. Every individual assumes a pseudopersonality that he unconsciously feels will advance his own self-interest. Some of us are more successful than others in submitting to the authority of the social image—that image of parental authority now grown large and powerful in our adult world. These are the people who stay out of mental hospitals and who are called "normal." Yet the same basic insecurity and fear underlies their behavior and the behavior of those within the hospital walls.

The two following stories illustrate the power of the social image, and the ambivalence of motivation characterizing the life of man.

Foreword

The two stories which follow were written under circumstances that call for a brief word of introduction. Some time ago the story of the coward was written, and the author of it said he would like to submit it. Another contributor was present by chance, and in the discussion that followed our reading it the question arose as to whether the coward in the story was really a coward—whether the story embodied the last word in the psychology of the coward. The writer of the first story felt that the coward in question *was* a coward and that that was all there was to it. The other felt that there were no basic differences between so-called cowardice and so-called courage, that these distinctions are born of social prejudices to which the individual is unconsciously too early subordinated and that both reactions indicated but a differentiation and separation among the common elements within a single personality. Feeling inadequate to explain in ordinary terms what he meant, he offered the suggestion that what was needed to complete the story of cowardice was the story of courage, and concluded by saying that he himself would essay the task. A few days later he brought in his story of "The Hero." Needless to say, while both stories are imaginative, they represent in broad lines the subjective experiences of the respective authors.

THE COWARD

As Bobby stepped out of the schoolhouse door a swift panic of fear seized him. He shrank back into the protecting shelter of the big entrance. Yes, Tiny was waiting for him. And Tiny had said that he was "going to beat him up"!—that "no other fellow had any right to carry his girl's books home except himself." Even at this distance the small figure of Tiny, who was at least a head shorter than Bobby, assumed the menacing proportions of an ogre. He could see this "ogre" making extravagant gestures to the small group of satellites that surrounded him by the

gate, and their nods of encouragement and admiration
threw panic into Bobby's heart. There was no doubt that
Tiny was mad and it could be plainly seen that he wasn't
going to waste any time in carrying out his threat when
once the offender appeared.

What could he do? How to escape the disgrace which
was sure to be his? He turned hurriedly and started back
to his schoolroom. He would erase the other blackboard
for his teacher, Miss Black. It might be that Tiny would
go. With breathless haste he rushed for the room. But
the door was locked. Miss Black must have already gone
to turn in the day's report to the principal. What must
he do? His scared little mind feverishly considered means
of escape--escape to home, where he knew he would be
safe.

As he lay there, crouched in a corner, he heard someone coming. It might be he. No, Tiny surely wouldn't
dare to come in the schoolhouse after him. It couldn't
be. But suppose he did find him there! With a sobbing
little cry he ran to the back of the hall and jumped out
of a low window. Scrambling to his feet, he peered about
him anxiously. No one was in sight. An avenue of escape
now presented itself to him. He would keep in the
shadow of shrubbery and trees which grew in the grounds;
climb the back fence and take a roundabout way home.
With this thought, some of the assurance which had so
shamefully deserted him returned. He gathered together
his scattered books, made an ineffectual attempt to
straighten his clothes and after one more careful glance
around he started out under the trees.

The boy might easily have been mistaken for some
wild creature as he slyly slunk from tree to tree. Mud-
stained. clothes still awry, he was no longer Bobby but
simply a hunted beast whose only aim was to reach a

place of safety. At last he reached the fence. A smile almost lighted his face as he realized that he would soon be safe and home. He clambered over the fence and— almost fell into the midst of a group of boys coming down the street. Among them he recognized Jim and Ed, his classmates, as they ran up. Fearful and too tired to move, he lay there.

"What's the matter?" one shouted. "What are you doing coming over the back fence, Bobby?"

And then as Jim's eyes caught the fear-stricken look on Bobby's face, he said, "Yes, I know why. He's scared. Tiny told me he was going to get him for going with his girl. What you 'fraid about anyway—Tiny's a whole lot smaller than you are—"

Bobby, speechless and shamefaced, said nothing.

"He's a 'fraid cat, that's what he is," sneered Ed. "Why he wouldn't even fight if you kicked him." And to clinch his statement, Ed drew back his foot and kicked him. Bobby flashed to his feet and one might have supposed that instinct would have its way and he would defend himself. But only for an instant. A hot flush of shame mounting to his cheeks, he averted his head, and with eyes on the ground he started to hurry away.

"Uh-huh, I told yuh so; he's afraid. He's a coward, a coward, a coward." And Ed spat at him.

Bobby, overwhelmed by this final evidence of his degradation, gave way to sobs that shook his frame. The cries of "coward" rang in his ears as the weeping boy made his way home.

THE HERO

Roy, tall and handsome, and without the customary vanity that follows admiration, was leader among the boys. Whatever he said or did was accepted by the others as criterion. He was their hero. There was nothing unusual or noteworthy in this, at least so far as the boys were concerned. It just happened. Like his ease in skating or swimming or any of his many activities, it happened so simply that it was taken for granted. Roy was naturally heroic.

During his early childhood, Roy had a trait that would not ordinarily be considered as a preface to heroism. He was unable to play or do anything alone. Alone he would make the attempt to entertain himself but invariably he would lose interest, become apathetic and finally sit down and merely "think." When Jade, his frequent companion, would happen upon him during one of these thinking moods, he would rush forward eagerly as though escaping from some dreaded bogey. But such a trait could hardly be considered unusual. And unless one cared to consider that later on Roy fell desperately in love with Mary, the serious-minded "tomboy" of his class, and yet rarely spoke to her except as school activities made it necessary, there was nothing at all unusual in his early days that might be remembered in later years as having been significant. On the contrary, Roy was delightfully buoyant and companionable and always the first to devise some new play interest. He never stood apart from his playmates nor did they feel any difference when with him, though even in those early years he was foremost in all their play enterprises. And yet for all his distinction he was simply a boy among boys—natural and unspoiled.

But with Roy's entrance into school, his activities became specialized. The social environment differentiated him from others and his heroic traits rapidly took form. Among the schoolboys he soon became leader in the accepted sense of a superior in all their activities—in baseball and football and outdoor games generally. He would lead daringly through suffocating tunnels in the hay-mow and would be equally courageous in rescuing those who had become fear-stricken. He delighted to explore in distant wild places for new swimming holes, and was ever the first to reach out a helping hand in a moment of danger. Deep woods and lonely trails held an especial attraction for Roy and the camping expeditions were ever marked by his exploits.

Roy was even built on heroic lines. His presence in the gymnasium easily led one to think of the Greeks or of Michelangelo's "David." And one day a stranger, stopping to admire him, remarked: "That boy has personality"—meaning, I suppose, that some day he would be a "great man." There was always a pleasing grace in his manner that bore the imprint of things simple and close to the earth. Mothers especially delighted in the picture of Roy. Not only did his parents think of him as a "good boy"; the village in general held him up as exemplar. True there had been that one muddy fight in which he had thrashed Bill Clark unmercifully; but after the secret talk Roy had with his father it was tacitly agreed that Bill was "a bad sort" and Roy became more the hero than ever before. In fact parents encouraged their sons to associate with Roy, though the encouragement was hardly needed. For Roy was already popular among the boys. Even in school the boys looked up to him. There wasn't one who wouldn't have given his all to be as "bright as Roy." Though he wasn't a student in the ordinary sense, he seemed to move and think in a large way and win favor with his teachers. During his senior year in high school his oration, "Problematic Europe," was the amazement of the teachers as well as of the boys.

And yet, though Roy was so evidently heroic, there was beneath his outward composure a certain shyness, a silence, an unfulfilment, something that suggested the thinking moods enforced by aloneness during early childhood. One could not say that Roy was not social and yet he was markedly retiring without anyone realizing it fully. Though he went to "parties," he abhorred them. Though he was much in love with Mary, he never sought her. He had also grown to be very fond of Miss Pierce, the assistant principal, yet no one ever knew, not even Miss Pierce. He would go for lonely walks at night. And he would spend whole days alone in the woods. What he did there Roy himself hardly knew. He only knew that in the depths of the woods or walking lonely roads at night he felt curiously comforted. It was as if some constricting force were removed from him; and he felt only the rhythmic swing of his body and a certain oneness with the countryside made gentle by the covering of darkness. There would come to him then vague thoughts of his mother, of Mary and even Miss Pierce and of Jade.

With the spring term of Roy's senior year in high school there came an undercurrent of disquiet in his days. It seemed to extend to the boys and even to Miss Pierce and in a sense to the village. Perhaps it were more correct to say that the village was ill and Roy the symptom—Roy and Miss Pierce and the school. For Roy and Miss Pierce could hardly have been held accountable individually for the entanglement of their feelings and emotions. Each one would have gladly avoided the confusion and held himself correctly within the strict consensus of the village life. But something happened that could not be understood—something within the social fabric of the village— an unseen restriction upon spontaneity that pitted Roy and Miss Pierce against each other in a way that could not have occurred in a simpler, more unified atmosphere. Miss Pierce found herself unnecessarily solicitous for Roy, and Roy was baffled by his fierce resentment against one whom he liked. Miss Pierce had asked him to sing in the chorus, to take part in the play, and he had flatly refused before he knew what he had done. She asked him for the loan of his attractively bound botany specimens, for Roy was good at drawing and his botany work was illuminated with color sketches. But, approaching her sullenly, he threw the folder with a bang on her desk. And after school, he rushed off to the woods and, flinging himself against an oak tree, pressed his lips against the rough bark. Miss Pierce continued to ply him with mental embraces. One day, as she looked over his shoulder at his work, she put her hand over his but Roy suddenly jerked his head back against her breast and she walked away with tears in her eyes.

Among the boys Roy now became alternately tyrannical and indifferent. But, curiously, his tyranny was met with submission, and his indifference was looked upon as self-control. Yet in a very subtle way Roy passed his confusion to the other boys, and the atmosphere of the classroom became charged with an indefinable element of rebellion.

Miss Pierce went on with her school work as usual but found it difficult to hide her confused thoughts and feelings. She was a successful teacher and much liked, both in school and in the village. Full of enthusiasm and gaiety, she had always moved among the students as one of them, never tiring in her interest and helpfulness. Her present apathy, however, was quite apparent. Many thought her ill. And though the solicitous ones were

successfully met with a laugh and some gay remark about
spring fever, she had to struggle desperately at times to
keep back the tears. The sudden realization one day that
she was in love with Roy brought a certain relief. But it
was a relief she would gladly have foregone, for the con-
sequent fear entailed a greater burden than the previous
confusion. And though it was now clearer to her that
Roy was back of the suppressed laughter and lack of attention in the classroom, her observation only heightened
her confusion. She longed to talk with Roy. She felt that
she could not go on much longer. Desperation was added
to confusion, yet there was no one whom she could trust
unless it were Roy himself. But her fear and the thought
that Roy was but a boy of eighteen held her back. When,
however, she saw Roy slip one of the boys a piece of
paper, her instinct as a teacher intercepted and the
decision came more easily. She asked that the paper be
handed to her and requested that Roy talk with her after
school.

Alarmed but with outer composure, Roy made his
way slowly to the office. Miss Pierce was standing by the
window but sat down as he entered. On the desk before
her lay the paper—a roughly executed but pleasing likeness
of Miss Pierce and a small sketch of an oak tree. As
she began to speak the tears came to her eyes but she
went on in spite of her fear and trembling. "I have not
asked you here to punish you, Roy. I want to talk with
you. I want to talk of you and me. I want your help. It
came to me the other day, very clearly, that I am too fond
of you. I do not understand it. I do not wish it. I know
that my fondness for you stands in the way of my work
and my understanding of you. I have thought at times
that you were unjust to me. But you couldn't help it. I

was cruel to you. It is all wrong. I know of no one any-where to speak to. But it cannot go on. I will have to leave unless—" Roy neither moved nor spoke. He stared with wild eyes out of the window at the distant woods. Miss Pierce, sensing his fear, lost her composure and reached out her hand to him. Roy cringed. With a look of despair in her face, she sank back in her chair; and as she bowed her head in her hands, her body shook with fierce sobbing.

Roy continued to stand there—almost sullenly—in front of her desk. He looked furtively from Miss Pierce to the window and back to the sketch on the desk. He nervously rubbed his damp hands against his coat. The muscles of his face twitched with the agony of fear. Then very silently and slyly, his body bent forward on tiptoe, he reached for the doorknob and went out.

Outside the closed door, he stood with his arm half-raised over his head. One might have thought he was crying, but Roy never cried. With backward glances he started to move away from the door, but stopped. For long, long moments he stood there—thinking and think-ing—his body swaying slightly toward the closed door. He made a sudden start to go back—but turned sharply and rushed out of the building—running furiously toward the ball field where the boys were at practice and fretting in the absence of their leader.

Naturally there was a volley of questions. "Ah, cut it out," barked Roy, as he put on the catcher's mask. "It was nothing—I just don't like women teachers and I don't think they oughta teach—Jade, you pitch our side—Want to warm up a bit?—Atta boy, right over the marble—Hey, you fellows," he shouted irritably to the boys at practice, "Tighten up—Don't be so sloppy—What's-a-matter,

Beany?—Say you, look here—Can the rough stuff—Take center and keep your eyes on the game."

Roy had become fairly convincing with his gesture of maturity and his slang. There were times now when it even seemed difficult not to say he was a bully. But then —always admired, almost worshipped—his irritation was overlooked. Though a good pitcher, he nearly always caught, preferring to train others into pitching. It went along with his ease at marshaling the boys into action. But today he couldn't contain himself. At the first opportunity, between innings, he walked away from the boys to the far side of the field. Little Toby followed and when he whispered very respectfully that Mary had gone by just before he arrived, Roy was almost visibly confused. Within himself he was desperately upset about everything —Miss Pierce and Mary and himself and everything. Today was not the beginning. Some time ago as he passed Mary on the street and felt himself trembling all over, he stopped and thought: "Then this is love? This is why people marry—why children are—why I am?" And he went over again and again the long moody moments in his study—alone—wondering who he was and whether he was not a coward and stupid. "I am I," he would say to himself, touching his own body. "But who is that fellow down there in the street? Jade—yes—but who is he? When I lift my arm, why doesn't his go up?" And he planned and replanned to speak to Miss Pierce. But the more he planned the more he thought of planning, each thought demanding answer in thought until his thinking grew and heaped up like an ugly storm cloud. He thought of telling his mother the truth, but it dawned upon him that he didn't know what the truth was. With the thought that he couldn't speak to his mother, terror was added to his confusion and he tended more than ever to think of Mary.

Yesterday Mary's little sister had been playing "grown-ups" with his little sister. His sister wore Mary's blue dress. She seemed very beautiful. He watched her—fascinated. He trembled not a little at times and had to struggle to retain his composure. He even touched the dress once—very reverently. When the children were through playing, he hid the dress in his room—and wondered all day why.

He was wondering now. The picture held him bound. His thoughts raced furiously. But he got nowhere—Mary—Miss Pierce—Mother—Mary—If only he could be a child again—If only he could bury himself deep in the hay in the great barn—deep—deep. Toby nudged Roy with the catcher's mask he had dropped in his abstraction. The boys were waiting, shouting for him. Roy pulled himself together with such a violent jerk that Toby jumped back in fear. But, seeing his mistake, he ran laughing to the bats he was tending.

As Roy settled to his heels behind the batter, he exhorted the players with a stream of slang and the game started. Though confused and trembling inwardly he somehow made a go of things—he always did—and no one ever knew. From out of the general clatter of tongues, one could easily hear Roy's steadying voice. "Fine, Jade, old top—Take your time—Listen to me, Jade—Don't mind the ump—Just you and me, old Harp—Just you and me—Now, then, make it hum a tune—Atta boy, old Harpie."

The game over, Roy rushed home without a word. The boys were not surprised. Accustomed to accept his behavior as criterion, they tended more to imitate than to criticize him. They didn't even question.

Roy's mother heard him go to his study in the far attic but, busy with the evening meal, thought no more of it. Once in a while he did go to his room without his customary affectionate greeting. In her view he was very much a student of books and often peculiarly absorbed.

When Roy reached his room, he flung himself on the couch but, too confused to rest, he wandered around aimlessly—feverishly, as though dazed and yet with some vaguely defined objective. He thought again of Mary's blue dress. Going softly to the drawer where he had hidden it the day before, he took it out and placed it gently on the couch, caressing it as he smoothed the folds. He stood before it as in a trance, touching it occasionally with marked reverence. With a deep sigh he put the dress on and stood before the tall mirror. Long moments he stood there, gently caressing his body through the folds of Mary's dress. Then slowly walking to his rifle locker and taking out the revolver, he went back to the mirror and shot himself in the temple.

The village buzzed for days with the gossip of the tragedy, never suspecting the part that it itself had played.

Both these boys were attempting to measure up to what Dr. Burrow calls "a false image of authority which had replaced the authority that resides in the consistent correspondence between man's senses and the external world." Bobby was afraid and ashamed because the authority of the social image compelled him to fight, and he hated fighting. Roy was afraid and ashamed because the authority of the social image forbade him to have erotic dreams about a teacher or to love feminine clothes. It required that he live up to the standards of his pseudopersonality and be the pure-minded hero, with neither irresolution nor confusion. But his motivation, as that of his community, was ambivalent. His wishful fancies were as compulsive as his fear. In this impasse there was only one thing for "the hero" to do—run away.

When man has recognized the source of division within himself, and turned to the study of his own processes, the power of the social image we have now imposed upon ourselves will be broken. It will no longer be possible for man to evade his obligation to "see life steadily and to see it whole."

CHAPTER VII

The "I"-Persona

In most of the material presented thus far, emphasis has been placed upon the thrall of a secret, competitive mood that grips human beings at all times. As we have seen, man is largely divorced from his organic sense of the biologically fitting and unfitting response, especially as it applies to his relations with others of his kind. He is conditioned to a moral or "right-wrong" dichotomy of behavior which has no dependable values in respect to the survival and well-being of mankind. "Right" is identified with a sense of divisive, personal advantage, "wrong" with a sense of divisive, personal disadvantage. In his separate mood each individual therefore clings tenaciously to his sense of "right," and thus constructs an *image of himself that is biologically fictitious.* In the day-by-day living of the group gathered for the express purpose of studying man's social reactions, this separative mood was found to be universally dominant. It was found that our interrelational behavior is habitually motivated by self-interested emotion or affect, that it is shot through with prejudice, that each individual is continually prone to look away from himself, to blame other people or external conditions for his affective difficulties.

One of the students wrote an account of her secret ruminations expressive of this mood. If we are objective, each of us will recognize that behind his own jealously guarded fantasies is a mood identical with that of the writer of the sketch.

THE MENTAL CINEMA

At the Breakfast Table

"This talk of these people about the election is rather interesting. I wonder why they don't address *me!* John's argument is certainly weak and as for Bill, he doesn't have the faintest idea of what he is talking about. *I* certainly ought to know because I heard Senator M. say the other day that this platform has nothing behind it, besides, anybody can see that! The papers too are full of it."

My voice is louder and more convinced as the thought of what I have to say carries me on. A general excitement and irritation—finally—

"I'd like to know who's going to stop me from saying what I've got to say! I know what *I* think. Anyhow I don't care about the old platform or the election either!"

In a Streetcar

"That is certainly a very handsome man over there! I like the way he wears his hat. And his ears are so nice. Oh! he is looking at me! I wonder what it is about me that interests him so especially."

I look out of the window and pretend to be unconcerned.

"He's gotten off without another glance at me! Pooh! It wasn't worth while making any effort for him!"

In the House of a Friend

"I don't want Nora to see me prinking. I look unusually well today though. My gown is becoming and hangs in long sinuous lines fitting to me. But that makes no real difference! All I can think of is him!"

He is coming! I hear the door close.

"Oh! how I love him!"

He is talking to his sister, Nora. My look is far away. I have an angelic, Madonna-like expression—it must be most impressive. It is vague and mystical. . . . He and I are together walking, talking. Now we are skating in the moonlight—my hands in his, our bodies swinging with a measured rhythm. It is very lovely! It is very soothing! The picture is quite entrancing really!

"Did I hear him mention her name? What does he mean! How does he expect me to love him when he treats me this way!—No matter what he does, though, I will love him! I will be a martyr!"

Tears come to my eyes. Slowly my brow becomes knit.

"I must find some way to make him see he can't do this to *me*. If I commit suicide—*then* he'll be sorry! He'll notice me *then!*"

Thus the scene shifts from hour to hour and from minute to minute. And always I am the star performer occupying the center of the stage.

I am in the nursery, the focus of an admiring audience. Nurse and Mother think me cute and sweet. They think me cuter and sweeter than any other child. This after all is the constant moving picture and I the constant star performer occupying the center of the stage.

This mood of secret absolutism and self-interest nourishes the sovereign social image to which we all give allegiance.

Whether we are engaged in achieving "social success" or in devoting ourselves to our families, or in helping the poor and needy, the mood behind our behavior is always one of pre-occupation with the social image of the "I."

In phylobiology, the term "I"-persona has been given to this spurious image-personality which has replaced the biological identity of the individual as a coordinated member of an integrated species. The "I"-persona is not an isolated phenomenon in each individual. It is the systematization of affects and prejudices that characterizes human society throughout, and is reflected in the pseudopersonality of the individual.

For example, let us imagine a child born in New York, whose mother is English and whose father is descended from generations of New Englanders. Both parents are omnivorous readers. They have only a small income. The father is a man of wide and liberal views, but he is obliged to suppress his spontaneous interests because they clash with his rather narrow evangelical religion. The result of this frustration is that he suffers agonies from "nervous indigestion." Out of this background, and separated from his inherent feeling of continuity with his species, this child may grow up with the following set of prejudices that remain a part of his pseudopersonality until the day he dies: that frugality is one of the cardinal virtues, that only people who read a great deal are worth while, that those who despise Negroes are stupid, that the way to get on is to serve, that the English are the greatest people on earth, that a person suffering from repression is an object of love. And so on, and so on.

With this emotional baggage for his journey through life, he will automatically gravitate toward people in his community who hold prejudices identical with his own. And he will feel critical or patronizing or antagonistic toward those who do not share these prejudices. He will find all his prepossessions socially consolidated in the larger world outside his family. He will find organized philanthropies for serving the needy, reading clubs for acquiring the contents of as many books as possible, unions for acclaiming the virtues and proficiencies of the English, associations for eliminating racial bias, and any number of repressed people who will turn eagerly to him for love. Or he may adopt a negative attitude toward his conditioning and defy the family traditions. But in this case he only builds up another set of prejudices for which he will find corroboration in the outside world. Both attitudes, however, are equally the expression of the socially ubiquitous "I"-persona. The recognition that an ulterior, divisive motivation underlies seemingly benign, as well as overtly malicious conduct, was a most important step in the early stages of the group research.

Trained as we are in a "right-wrong" interpretation of human behavior, it is very difficult, it is almost impossible, for us to recognize that there are few exceptions to self-interested motivation in the so-called normal world. One thinks of the prophets, the martyrs, the great philosophers—all the servants of humanity whose selfless lives have been an inspiration to mankind. How can it be, one asks, that these high-minded men and women can be enmeshed in the same treacherous net that entangles the lives of ordinary men? But this very question springs from the divided mind of the "I"-persona. The noblest men are above us because we think them so. Their nobility is not something apart from us. It is the expression of a deep, inclusive feeling that is the heritage of every man, but from which we have turned away to worship at the shrine of a parochial deity called "I." Their nobility is our nobility. But they partake of our neurosis as well. Thoreau, delighting in the common joys of life, nevertheless wrote with lofty scorn of those whose way of life was not his. George

Washington was hot-tempered and swore like a trooper at his opponents. Florence Nightingale was a cold, ruthless tyrant toward anyone who stood in her way. Each had a program for pursuing a course that in his or her eyes was the only right one, and all who did not serve were dubbed iniquitous.

The truth is, we do not recognize the extent to which the ineptness in man's adaptation influences our reactions in every situation of our lives. Each of us plays the role of hero in a drama of his own devising. Each looks on at the role as he plays it. Sometimes we play it successfully; we are acclaimed and are pleased. At other times we cannot live up to the demands of the role, and then we are discouraged. But at all times we are both actor and audience.

The "I"-persona being a social systematization of affects, the community, too, is under the same compulsion. Its attitude toward the George Washingtons and the Florence Nightingales of history is a case in point. It sets up a hero on a pedestal and worships him. History is full of legendary supermen. In our contemporary life also we set up heroes who play their part in response to the mood-stimulus of the audience, and adopt a pose that sets them apart from and above the crowd. Man's affective mood is a reflex in which we all take part automatically without recognizing the puppet quality of our behavior.

Written at about the same time as the sketches presented in this book, the following statement by Dr. Burrow is interesting in this connection.

Through this projection of himself as hero, the individual necessarily becomes at the same time both actor and onlooker. But whether one is a hero to others or to himself, the underlying mechanism is the same. Whether the personality in question is an outstanding character of history or the introverted neurotic personality, there can be no hero without an audience. If one assumes an image of himself, there is necessarily that part of himself from which his image is projected. If one assumes mentally the rôle of hero, one necessarily assumes mentally the rôle of hero-worshipper. If the individual performs a part, he also observes himself in the performance of it. If one part of him acts, the other looks on at his own acting. In this way the individual acquires a twofold basis; the one personal, the other social. I mean by this that in holding an image attitude toward himself, he necessarily holds a social or opposite attitude toward himself. But the individual's division is further reduplicated. For the same image that divides him from himself at the same time divides him from others. The same division that is personal within him of necessity becomes by extension social also. It is precisely this division of the individual into actor and onlooker, and its extension within the social mind, to which we owe the birth of the hero. ("The Heroic Rôle—An Historical Retrospect." *Psyche*, London, 1926, Vol. VI, p. 44.)

One of the principal aims of group analysis was to turn the attention of the participants upon the subjective state accompanying such walking shadows as those depicted in this passage from Dr. Burrow's writings. In this connection, the reader may be interested in a letter from a student who had submitted himself to the discipline of such a training, and wrote out of his experience.

LETTER TO THE EDITOR

The Editor of Mental Health
DEAR SIR:
Judging from the tone of your Journal you will perhaps

welcome a statement written from the point of view of a victim of a nervous disorder. To my mind such a statement—in so far as it is helpful at all—should mean much more to other sufferers than the most learned opinion of the best-trained physician. For in the degree in which a patient is capable of a real understanding of his condition, he—better than anyone—knows what is going on within his own personality.

It so happens that the successive periods of depression and elation to which no doubt every one is more or less prone, are in my case so concentrated and severe as to make existence for roughly six months of each year a painful burden. To illustrate, through a series of years I have during the periods of elation succeeded somehow or other in establishing in the minds of those who know me a sense of an ability for constructive work. During the periods of depression this reputation faces me constantly in the form of the question, "Well, what interesting piece of work is keeping you busy?" I stare, wonder how the unoccupied being I now am could ever have inspired such a question, and in an ill-concealed panic hunt for a means of escape.

Worn out with the pain of the oft-repeated experience I have almost entirely withdrawn from activities that formerly inspired me with great enthusiasm. This has added, if possible, to what I may call the normal depression, until the burden has reached a stage that seems almost to stun my native sensibilities.

Needless to say, throughout each year I have accepted these recurrent periods of depression and elation with the greatest possible degree of seriousness. Recently, however, an unexpected challenge has cast a doubt upon their validity. It happened that in what may be considered an insignificant situation I had a momentary flash of insight into the artificiality of the depression—into the fact of its being a coating so to speak, laid over the personality that is the real "I." There followed automatically the thought that in this case the elated "I" must be equally an unreal being. Carried to its logical conclusion, I am gradually beginning to realize the helpful possibilities that lie within this experience. Perhaps the most constructive piece of work that I can undertake is a grasping of the significance of these unreal moods that have in the past seemed real. If with the help of the increasing number of those interested in such problems I can pierce the unreality of the veil separating me from myself, not I alone shall be the gainer. At least I sense vaguely the possibility of an opportunity for constructive work in this subjective situation that is of greater importance than those objective undertakings that formerly aroused my interest. If in this thought I am seeing clearly, it may be worth while to bring it to the attention of others possibly in a similar situation. It is for this reason that I am writing this letter.

The following article also gives an arresting picture of the split personality as felt from "the inside."

YESTERDAY AND TODAY

Yesterday I had a "brainstorm." I don't quite know how it started. All of a sudden my whole life seemed to fall to pieces. The teaching I was doing was a fake, the things I believed were not true, my friends were hypocrites and cowards, and I was as bad as they. The world was a horrible place; people were starving and cold while I lived in plenty. My income burned me; it did not belong to me, for I had not earned it. It seemed a criminal offense to keep it any longer. In the intervals between my tears I spent the morning wondering how I could get the money I have back to the people who really had earned it, and composing imaginary letters to the New School of Social Research asking for advice on the subject. Ordinary "charity" would not do at all—since the money did not belong to me how could I give it to anyone? And yet something fair and just had to be done at once.

Yet even in my excited state the little imp at the back of my mind kept his calm cold eye on my proposed course of conduct. "Yes, you're awfully interested in creating a sensation by handing over your stock to the employees of the Pennsylvania Railroad," whispered the imp, "but I notice that you are rather vague about the hard work of earning your living that is to follow. Why don't you dope out how that is to be done? Are you going to work in a factory? Or scrub floors? You *might* look for a self-supporting job now, if you are so crazy for one, and give up your money after you have made a few practical arrangements." But all these suggestions were washed away in tears for the misery of the world and my own unworthiness.

Then suddenly, click, the tears stopped as if they had been turned off by a faucet. The clock reminded me that I had to give a music lesson, and that it was time to cover up the traces of grief. So I dried my eyes and went through the motions of teaching for an hour. When the lesson was over the grief was gone. Where did it go? Goodness knows. But today the brainstorm has vanished, and I am as "sane" as usual. That is to say I am walking around with a smile on my face, instead of lying on my bed weeping, and the usual stream of self-satisfied revery is running through my head. "How well I have been playing golf lately! My stroke is extraordinary for a person of my size, particularly when you think that I can only play once a week. . . . Wasn't that an interesting visit to that beautiful little churchyard where all my ancestors are buried? It isn't everybody in America who has seven generations of ancestors buried in one churchyard. . . . That child I teach is really doing extraordinarily well, she is quite a genius. . . ."

"Oh, bosh!" interrupts the outraged imp. "You know none of your pupils can play for a cent! And what is all this about ancestors? I thought you called yourself a Socialist."

But my revery ignores these remarks and goes gaily on. "Perhaps I can go horseback riding again on Sunday. It *is* expensive, of course, and I haven't much money after paying my bills, but I guess I'll do it anyhow. . . . Gee, I'm glad I'm not in such a blue fit as I was yesterday! Whatever possessed me to want to give my money to the people who earned it? They would only get about a tenth of a cent apiece, and if they got more they would spend it on getting drunk, or something. I certainly was crazy yesterday, but I'm all right again today."

"Perhaps you're just as crazy today, if not more so," suggests the imp. Then, seeing that this question is likely to cause another panic, he adds sadly, "Don't worry! You won't be put in any insane asylum. Everybody else is just as crazy as you are today."

Only rarely are we able to achieve even so fleeting a sense of the artificiality of our moods as is disclosed in these sketches. Usually we accept as perfectly valid the most startling shifts of mood, our only concern being to justify them to ourselves and to other people. The "I"-persona is a brilliantly resourceful director of the show in which each of us "struts and frets his hour." It can almost always invent an impressive disguise for our self-interested characterizations. The little comment entitled "Query" is concerned with one of these disguises.

QUERY

Is there any basis in fact for the popular distinction we make so glibly between pride on the one hand and false pride on the other? There is no limit to the things upon which we seize as justification for our feelings of pride— physical beauty, material wealth, manual skill, mental ability, business success, goodness, badness even. None of us is so lowly that he has not a standard to which he can fasten the banner that is his pride, thing of shreds and patches though it be. But what is at the bottom of this pride other than the quite personal satisfaction of convincing oneself that he is from some point of view superior to his neighbors?

In the use of the term "false pride" there is the implication of a certain validity, a certain worth-whileness in the ordinary brand. But as a matter of reality there is no difficulty to be found in the attempt to reduce the two to their common terms.

One is proud of the position he occupies, let us say. In other words the position is one from which he can look down upon those about him and impress upon them the fact that he is a superior person. In such a situation he takes his pride quite seriously and does not want to see it for what it is—merely a barrier which he places between himself and those about him. In so far as he is proud, others must be humble in his presence. In so far as he can pose as superior, others must consider themselves inferior in comparison with himself.

In time there comes a shifting of the scenes, and with the turning of the spotlight upon another portion of the stage, he finds himself in the shadow. But at all costs he must keep his pride, and with a realization that in the eyes of others there is no justification for it, it assumes a different aspect and now it bears the label "false." But always there is the same situation that is responsible—namely, a situation that is none other than the same old barrier which he erects to keep himself apart from his fellows.

Is it not possible that innately we have a sense of the fact that fundamentally there is no justification for our feelings of pride under any conditions—and for this reason we have developed the popular distinction to blind ourselves to the truth that all pride is false?

How far removed from the child's joyous acceptance of life is this dreary preoccupation with the appearance we are making? Judged from the standpoint of the organism's fundamental potentialities, we are a set of dull automatons. Is it any wonder that we are ever seeking to assuage the pain of this breach in organic integrity by means of some nepenthe of our own contriving? The essay that follows speaks of an aspect of man's restless search for respite from his inward pain.

"VACATE—TO MAKE EMPTY" (WEBSTER)

"Ten more days and we'll be free
From this school of miser-ee,
No more pencils, no more books,
No more teachers' ugly looks."

My friend smiled at the youngsters from the superiority of her forty summers, and I smiled with her. Of

course we used to sing it too—but we didn't think it was
doggerel then. Now we are grown up—adult.

But are we? Isn't there something of the same mood
in our own vacations? My friend rejected the idea as
preposterous, though I had already recalled the numerous
colleges and universities of the land where thousands of
students are frenziedly "cramming" for their "finals,"
consoled meanwhile by a vision of the absolute freedom
that will follow commencement day. I quoted the devotee
of higher education who, when asked what he expected to
read during the summer, replied, "Read? Hell! I'm not
going to open a book till next October unless I flunk this
exam and have to bone Horace."

My friend thought that an unfair sample, so I suggested that we consider instead the countless offices where
Jones and Smith and Brown are debating the relative
merits of trips through the Great Lakes and a fortnight
at Atlantic City, all the while secretly envying "the boss"
his trip abroad.

"But surely," protested my friend, "people have to
have time to play—to do just what they want to!"

"Then I can only say that it seems to me that they
have a sorry time of their play."

Her denial was instantaneous. "Oh, you're wrong!
On the contrary they have a gorgeous time. Why, last
summer I—"

But I had already heard all about last summer at least
a dozen times, and to spare myself another recital I interrupted, "Yes, I know, I saw thousands of vacationists
myself last summer. They were packed together on the
beaches and they held down rockers on the porches of
every small-town hotel. They filled the Pullmans and
the steamers, and their cars made a steady procession along

the highways. But their faces! Did you take a single good look at their faces? Some of them had the do-or-die expression you might expect on a battlefield and others looked just plain bored. These people were dancing and swimming and doing all of the joyous things that belong to a genuine vacation, but the only signs of merriment I noticed were occasional bursts of irresponsible, giggly laughter. Yet in the fall, when they all came back to town, not one of them would have dared admit to himself or to anyone else that his vacation had been a dreadful flop. Instead, everybody began telling everybody else what a glorious summer he had had. I've done it myself."

"I suppose," said my friend sarcastically, "that you are advocating working twelve months a year and *never* taking a vacation. You can't interest me in anything like that."

"Hardly that," I replied, "but it does seem a bit stupid to try to crowd six weeks full of a good time and then not really have a good time; to work like a fiend for ten months in order to forget all about work for eight weeks. It occurs to me that it's not so much our vacations that are at fault as our whole attitude toward our work and our play. We never stop to ask 'What *is* work and what *is* play,' but we assume that whatever isn't work is play and vice versa. One would hardly think of a musician taking a vacation from music! It's a part of his life. He might travel or have periods when he would practice less but I can't imagine his saying, 'I don't want to hear another musical note for three months.' And a baby! No one ever thought of a baby taking a vacation. Vacations don't begin until one starts to go to school. Yet I doubt whether there is any time when the human organism is working harder than during the years of infancy."

My friend was becoming restless—as restless as I had been when it was first suggested that my own vacations were not all that I believed them to be. Suddenly she turned to me: "By the way—didn't you say you had a friend who had taken the trip from here to California by boat? You know they're giving me five weeks off this summer and I thought—"

I looked at my friend's face. It had the set expectancy of the confirmed vacationist. Already she was on her way to California.

From the street corner below came the voices of children, singing—

"No more Latin, no more French,
No more sitting on a hardwood bench.
Ten more days and we'll be free
From this school of miser-ee."

The division within the motivation of man today is a condition out of which issues the continual quarreling that characterizes our interrelations. Families, composed of individuals each secretly ensconced in his own niche of "rightness," are a prey to antagonism that flares up at any moment. The following vignette presents a conversation in which the latent mood of conflict is continually breaking forth.

BY THE FIRESIDE

MOTHER—I must say I think Ohio is perfectly right in refusing to pass the Child Labor Amendment if it will (as they say) prevent a farmer from requiring his children to work on his farm until after they are sixteen years of age. Too much idleness is a very bad thing for children.

FATHER—The law says eighteen, not sixteen. Poor

people can't afford to keep their children in school until they are eighteen years old.

DAUGHTER—Oh no, Father—I'm sure the law says sixteen.

FATHER—It's nothing of the kind—it's eighteen.

DAUGHTER—I heard one of the speakers at the Open Forum say or I read some place that the age was sixteen. The person also said that getting the word round among the public that the age limit was eighteen was only propaganda put out by the mill owners who profit by child labor. They spread this propaganda in order to prejudice the public against the Amendment so that it will be easier to defeat it. I think children have a right to an education in this land of plenty.

FATHER—Well, I don't know that an education is helping you much. I had to leave school when I was twelve years old. I'm making a living and that's more than you re doing.

DAUGHTER—Yes, and I've heard you regret your lack of an education many times.

FATHER—Well, I know that the age is eighteen and I don't care a hang what the Open Forum speaker says. Senator Pat Harrison of Mississippi, in tonight's paper, distinctly states that the age limit is eighteen years. I guess you wouldn't dispute the word of a United States Senator in a public statement, would you?

DAUGHTER—I don't care what Pat Harrison says. The only way to get the truth of the matter is to write for a copy of the proposed amendment and see for yourself. I wouldn't believe Pat Harrison, the Open Forum speaker or anyone else. All men are liars and women too, myself included. I've never met anyone who didn't lie when pushed hard enough.

FATHER—I resent that statement.

MOTHER—You express yourself too freely and too emphatically. People don't like to hear such things, particularly if they are true.

DAUGHTER—Well, why shouldn't I say what I think? You don't either of you have to think as I do, it's only a matter of opinion. Do you want me to sit with my mouth shut all the time?

MOTHER—I haven't noticed you doing that much of the time. Besides, I'm not sure the things you say are really your own thoughts. They sound pretty much to me like a rehash of what you hear other people say.

FATHER—And I'm tired of your Open Forum jargon.

DAUGHTER—Oh well, why quarrel anyway? Let's change the subject.

FATHER—All right. I see Jack Dunning has married Lucy Tucker. Who is she?

DAUGHTER—Movie actress. I wonder how long it will last. Not long, I'll bet, before he'll be wishing he'd never seen her and be casting sheep's eyes around in other pastures.

FATHER—Oh, I don't know about that. Prizefighters are not famous for their infidelities.

DAUGHTER—Well, maybe they're not. Perhaps I was just thinking of men in general, and women, too. It can never be any other way as long as women are satisfied to live according to the man-made marriage and divorce laws, to look on themselves as chattels of the male. No wonder men get sick and tired of their wives. They put the bitters in their own sweets. We all get sick and tired of anything we have too much of, makes no difference how nice it is.

FATHER—Well, it's a blame good thing all the women haven't as crazy ideas as you have.

DAUGHTER—Not much use changing the subject, was it, Dad?

FATHER—No, I'll be hanged if it was—not with you around anyway. A body never knows what to avoid in order to keep out of a row with you, for you change your mind every other day.

DAUGHTER—I'd rather do that than be as "sot" in my ways as you are.

FATHER—Oh, is that so!

MOTHER—I feel like screaming. I'm in hot water whenever you two are together. It's just like being between the devil and the deep blue sea.

DAUGHTER—I'm sorry, Mother. Seems like we're just bound to fight, whether it's over the Child Labor Amendment or Jack Dunning. Good night. Thank God at least one can go to sleep.

These people are discussing important public questions in which they are presumably interested. Yet their remarks show that they are really not interested. They have not troubled to acquaint themselves accurately with the elementary facts of the situations they are talking about. Each of them is merely grabbing an opportunity to express his own sense of rightness and his antagonism to the other members of the family. The "I"-persona is everlastingly right and everlastingly blind and everlastingly fighting for its own prerogatives. And it is inevitable that when this family situation is enlarged, when the "I"-personae of sovereign nations clash, then we have the paroxysm of war. Today, however artificial, the "I"-persona is the ruler of the life of man. Until man can bring himself to withdraw from his secret drama of hero-worship—that is, worship of his own image—and look at his behavior with objective clarity, we must go on fighting one another. As the following essay emphasizes, however, man's inclination is toward the concealment of his social malady.

THE INCURABLE MALADY

The disease that afflicts us most is the disease we do not want to rid ourselves of. The disorder the doctor is powerless to remedy is the disorder we hug to ourselves and secretly hide from him. There are diseases the nature of which is nothing else than the desire to keep their existence secret. As the disease I am bent on keeping secret must under no conditions be discovered by anyone else, naturally there is small chance that anyone else will relieve me of it. It is the secret of the disease of the drug-addict, for example, that no one must know the secret of his drug-addiction. The disease that is his secret is the secret of his disease. But how infinitely more illusive must be a disease the secret of which is lodged in a social compact among many individuals!

There is a malady prevalent among us that is unrecognized but of exceeding virulence. This malady is social. It is mental. Not only does it invade the tissues of the individual but it permeates the entire social organism. And it is as insidious as it is obstinate. For the nature of this disorder is the attitude of secret concealment of it on the part of all the individuals who share it. This social disorder is our obsessive self-interest and its secret maintenance by each of us at the expense of the interest of others. This obsessive self-interest or interest in one's own advantage must be kept secret because the advantage upon which it feeds is necessarily the advantage it has secretly obtained through the disadvantage of others. For secret self-advantage is of its nature parasitic. It can only find nourishment for itself in the disadvantage it secures over others. Such servile self-interest must, of course, be kept secret. For obviously others will not furnish the soil necessary to my advantage if they discover the disadvantage that must concomitantly accrue to themselves. Hence the necessity that the disorder of my self-advantage be kept secret from others. And what is true of me is, of course, equally true of everyone who shares in this social epidemic of secret self-advantage. As I must secure a secret advantage from others, so others must secure a secret advantage from me. For others, as well as I, must supply the soil of disadvantage that will afford their neighbors the secret self-advantage which they crave and which they, no less than I, are bent upon securing for themselves.

A recital of my personal ills must be attended by a secret pretense that my captive listener is really interested to hear them. He must not know that I know that he is fairly on tenterhooks in his eagerness to be off upon his own advantageous enterprises. The debts I incur out of love for my family must not be recognized as the secret price I pay for my reputation for successful standing in the community. My underpaid clerk or servant must not know that I know that he is underpaid. Conversely, my employer must not know that I know he is a driving monopolist. As employer I must on no account let it be known that my amity and my good will are my personal bid for secret self-advantage. As servant I must not let it be known that my secret self-comfort, couched in the thought, "Well, things are as they are," is but a sop to my fears, and that my cry of injustice is backed by a secret greed for an advantage over him who has pushed me to disadvantage. The nations that fight for what is right must keep secret from one another what they really know—that each is fighting for a hidden wrong and that his real "right" is but the secret of his private interest and monopoly.

Here indeed is a serious disease for which no "remedy" is by any chance obtainable—the disease that is our secret self-advantage. For it is precisely the subtle ruse of this disease that is its distinction—the ruse whereby each of us refuses to discover a remedy for it. This is the inviolate secret of our social malady, and in accordance with it each of us hopes secretly to obtain the largest advantage for himself through his self-concealment of it. Hence it is as futile as it is unwelcome to look for help. For there is no doctor who can relieve such a disorder. The doctor shares it with us. His secret advantage feeds no less than our own upon the disadvantage of others, and he, therefore, like ourselves must keep the secret of his advantage as we must keep secret our own.

Clearly, the physician competent to the relief of this widespread social disorder—a disorder due to our widespread individual secrecy and self-advantage—cannot be an individual like ourselves, sharing like ourselves in a like social malady. Clearly, only a societal mind that includes in its social survey both physician and patient will be competent to outroot this widespread social infirmity dependent, as it is, upon our widespread individual secrecy.

This disease of society with its symptomatic expressions in our industrial possessivism and in our social paroxysms of war, based as they are upon the ever-present secret claims of one individual upon another, can only be envisaged rationally by the societally united mind of the community as a whole. These disorders of our common social organism will then be as clearly recognized clinically as we now recognize clinically the disorders of the individual insane.

Today our individual concealment of our social self-advantage begins occasionally to break the threads of its security. But for any effective realization of this social malady there is needed a social recognition of the self-concealments that comprise it—there is needed a common recognition of a common, social maladjustment through a common disclosure of our individual differentiation and secrecy.

The social recognition of man's neurosis will inevitably involve a revolution in man's thought and feeling. The revolution will be as unsettling to our habituations as was the recognition of the germ origin of disease to the habituations of an earlier generation. When the bacteriologists first advanced the theory that there was an identifiable agent responsible for all typhoid cases, or all smallpox cases, or all tuberculosis cases, most physicians tried to laugh them to scorn. It was deemed a ridiculous idea that there could be a community approach to such diseases. But as the bacteriological data accumulated and were gradually accepted by physicians and laymen, legislation was enacted to protect the health of the community. The livelihood of thousands of people was threatened by the new orientation—farmers whose cows were tuberculous, owners of unsanitary tenements, shopkeepers selling loose milk, or dispensing drinks in unclean containers. Yet in spite of their impassioned protests "the societally united mind of the community" addressed itself to the task of controlling infectious disease at its source, with the result that many of these diseases have been practically eliminated from the civilized world.

There is no gainsaying the fact that in grappling with the "I"-persona of man we are faced with a large order. For each individual it involves the repudiation of his cherished image-identity. This is not a painless procedure, or one to which the individual lends ready support. Any questioning of the "I"-persona and its arbitrary system of rightness is fought tooth and nail, as the rigid resistances of the laboratory students amply testified. But phylobiological investigations reveal that there exists a constructive force within man the power of which greatly exceeds his individualistic strivings. This force is the expression of a native cohesiveness and integration running through and primarily motivating the behavior of the species. Man will be able to tap this force when he has applied the appropriate technique to his divisive behavior. Then the most socially communicable and destructive of all diseases—the disordered feeling of the "I"-persona—will be controlled at its source, and a new era of health and constructiveness will be opened to mankind.

CHAPTER VIII

Man as a Unitary Organism

So far we have dealt principally with the symptoms of a racial dissociation as they were observed in the early years of the phylobiological researches. We have focused upon these negative or disordered features in man's behavior because a full awareness of them represented an essential phase in the development of a technique for their study and control. Before the inauguration of Dr. Burrow's pioneer investigations there had been no awareness of the nature or the scope of the behavioral disorder affecting mankind. It was thought that disturbance in the realm of man's thinking and feeling was restricted to isolated individuals with "nervous and mental" disorders. Contrasted with these unfortunate digressors was the world of normality which was supposedly composed of individuals whose thinking and feeling was healthy. The specialist dealing with human behavior saw the symptoms of disorder clearly enough in the individual patient. He recognized the obvious anxiety and conflict, the blatant projection of affect upon others, the self-centered systematization of feeling and thinking. But he had no suspicion that these same disordered processes were present in a socially systematized and approved form within his own organism and throughout "normality" generally. His inevitable procedure was an attempt to restore his "wayward" patient to a mode of feeling, thinking, and acting in line with the feeling, thinking, and acting of the wider community. In other words, "normal" behavior was accepted as healthy behavior.

As we have seen, Dr. Burrow early questioned this gratuitous assumption. Observations made in his psychoanalytic practice caused him to suspect that "normal" behavior was merely our accustomed or generally accepted conduct, with little reference to its intrinsic fitness. We saw in Chapter II that in order to submit the question to experimental test he assembled a group of associates, students and patients—normal and neurotic, professional and lay—and embarked upon an intensive program of group analysis. These group-analytic studies showed that our "normal" social behavior is not healthy social behavior. They showed that the behavior of both normal and neurotic is determined by identical elements of egocentricity, of emotional projection, of wishful thinking and feeling, of prejudice and bias. As stressed in Chapter VI, the standards of "normality" are transient and mutable. They differ from culture to culture and, in the same culture, from time to time and from one circumstance to another. Judged by our present behavioral standards, it is normal to hoard superfluous wealth and property, to enter into cutthroat competition, to satisfy one's greed, to wish to control the lives and destinies of others. Moral conflict within the individual, the conflict between desires and principles, between so-called material and spiritual values, between the lusts of the body and the yearnings of the soul—these are "normal" expressions. "Normal" also are those myriad reactions of interindividual conflict and dissension—discord between man and wife, father and son, sister and brother, lover and beloved. At the most massive level of "normal" human interaction is the deadly and implacable conflict between vast aggregates of people with differing ideological concepts and forms of government—between totalitarianism and liberalism, between Communism and democracy.

Being part and parcel of the normal fabric, we constantly tend to enjoy the immunity of normality and to overlook our common behavioral disease. Participating in a condition that is socially ubiquitous, we do not perceive the disorder that it represents. We may draw an analogy from a situation that existed in certain parts of the South several generations ago in respect to a specific physical disease. Malaria was very widespread at that time, and in mosquito-infested coastal and swamp areas it was not unusual for whole communities to be stricken with it. The inhabitants of these communities came to accept the chills and fever, the malaise and lack of energy, as a matter of course. Since everyone had these symptoms, people hardly regarded them as evidence of illness. They accepted as a necessary and normal part of their lives that which was in reality disease and a heavy burden upon their organisms. They had now only the feeling of the disease. They had forgotten how it felt to have an organism abounding with energy and health.

So it is with us today in respect to our human relations. We accept our conflicts and antagonisms, our prejudiced thinking, our disfigured feeling as natural and intrinsic features of human behavior. Being strangers to the joy and fullness of function native to man as an organismically coordinated species, we are habitually oblivious of our social disorders in feeling and thinking. As things stand, man does not recognize his malady, does not realize that his relationship to his fellows is obstructed and disordered. He does not relate the dramatic symptoms of his global illness to an immediate and continuous dislocation within his feeling and his physiology.

It is imperative, therefore, that in this book we should stress social symptomatology. It is necessary that we become fully aware of the discrepancies in our normal behavior and that we regard them as symptoms of a disorder affecting the feeling life of mankind throughout. Man needs to have his behavioral illness brought vividly before him. He needs to feel in his very vitals that his behavior is disordered. There must be such a background before his interest can be compellingly aroused in a discipline that will restore basic principles of behavioral health—principles that are as intrinsic to the organism of social man as are principles of physiological health to the organism of the single individual.

Even in the early years of Dr. Burrow's psychoanalytic practice, long before his introduction of the group method of analysis, his attention had turned to a unitary, coordinating principle characterizing the primary behavior of man. This principle he traced to the first interrelational experience of the race—the prenatal contact between the organisms of infant and mother. This physiological experience of oneness is not lost at birth. Dr. Burrow found that a subjective continuity, an organic bond grew out of this preconscious phase of development, and he called this unified mode the principle of primary identification. Here there is no sense of space or time, no urge to struggle and attain, no emulation or sense of otherness. The motivation is basic and unified, and a profound harmony pervades the relation. Through his observation of self-contained moods in neurotic patients, through his analysis of dreams, through noting various intuitive expressions of poets and other artists, he became aware that a vestige of this biologically fulfilling experience is the basis of certain aspects of human feeling everywhere.

Dr. Burrow first presented his thesis of a unitary preconscious mode of experience in a paper, "Psychoanalysis and Life," read before the New York Academy of Medicine in

1913. The concept enlarged and developed in importance for him through the years. In speaking of it in *The Biology of Human Conflict—An Anatomy of Behavior, Individual and Social* (New York: The Macmillan Company, 1937), he says:

> As we consider this primary mode of subjectivity that characterizes the pre-self, we find it to be a non-libidinal, a pre-objective phase of the organism's development. Upon analysis we find also that many subjective experiences occurring in the individual's later development indicate their close relationship to this primary preconscious phase of the organism. . . . In the fleeting intimations of this later behavior in which there is carried over into adult life the organism's primary mode of identification and unity, there is no opposite, no like and dislike, no "me" versus "you," no "right" and no "wrong." On the contrary, the sensations and reactions belonging to this mode give intimation of a subjectively quieter, more collected mood (p. 76).

According to Dr. Burrow, this preconscious identity of mother and infant is the forerunner of a wholeness or solidarity in feeling and thinking that natively characterizes man as a species. This racial solidarity or cohesion existed prior to the development of man's competitive and divisive impulse, and it operates constantly to conserve the race. It was ever Dr. Burrow's effort to emphasize the presence of this primary health and wholeness of feeling, and to free it for its inherent integrative function. But for years it was not found possible to tap the unifying force inherent in the phylo-organism of man. The "I"-persona and the social neurosis blocked access at every point. It was not until the researches entered the field of the physiological processes underlying affect that Dr.

Burrow discovered and perfected a technique for implementing the great constructive force represented in man's racial solidarity of feeling. In these final chapters we shall consider Dr. Burrow's development of the concept of phylic solidarity as it applies to man's behavior, and give supporting evidence from other fields of inquiry.

Medicine and biology have, of course, long recognized a principle of integration and homogeneity extending throughout the human species. Physiologists, embryologists, and neurologists have shown in their detailed studies how the different parts and organs of the body are coordinated to form a total, functioning structure. They have described the subtle interweaving of chemical factors and nervous impulses which serves to secure the balance of the organism as a total unit. The part-functions are so correlated and integrated in the configuration of the organism-as-a-whole that life is maintained, that growth and adaptation to the environment become possible.

This basic integration within the organism is the same the world over; the healthy functioning of the lungs and kidneys is everywhere identical. Medicine recognizes that, if an individual is to be healthy, his physiology must adhere to the pattern of function typical of the species throughout. Similarly, physical diseases, such as pneumonia or nephritis, are described in medical writings with no qualification as to racial group or geographic location. Physicians treat diseases in accordance with common basic principles, irrespective of the country, race, or creed of the patient. Successful treatment is based on the phylic consistency of structure and function.

Medicine and biology, however, have so far failed to recognize the need for such a phylic norm of healthy functioning in the sphere of man's interrelational behavior. They have not searched for a basic principle of coordination and solidarity

underlying the social life of man. This is the task undertaken
by the phylobiological studies here reported. From their beginning they were directed toward the development of a valid
norm of health in respect to social behavior. The early phases
of the investigations dramatically disclosed the inadequacy of
normality to represent healthful and whole living. They
equally presaged the establishment of a norm that would represent behavioral health—a norm that would rest upon a principle
of continuity and coordination running through the species
and binding it together as an organismic whole. Writing at
the time of the group studies cited in this book (1923), Dr.
Burrow says:*

> We need to take account of the original, racial soli-
> darity of man's consciousness and to consider the
> interpenetrations of common instincts and habits that
> originally ramified throughout the undifferentiated mental
> tissue of our common species, knitting its contributing
> elements into a unitary, homogeneous organism. We need
> to form a clearer image of the uniform, coördinated *one-
> mindedness*, of this primordial, "multi-cellular" organism
> that was man. In brief, we need to recognize the
> *individual* that was originally the aggregate consciousness
> of the race. For, to consider man's phylogeny at this
> period of his evolution is to consider a unitary organism.
> It is to break through the prejudice of the separative mode
> of individual men and reckon immediately with the
> unified principle of consciousness as a whole, from which
> only later there diverged the separative elements repre-
> sented in the dissociated units we ourselves now comprise,

---

* The *Social Basis of Consciousness—A Study of Organic Psychology* (New
York; Harcourt, Brace & Co., 1927), p. 160. Quoted by permission of the
publisher.

but which unified principle survives to-day unaltered in the common unity of our confluent societal personality.

And again:

It is the inherent urge actuating this common societal impulse, as contrasted with the narrower motives of separateness and self, that is envisaged in an organismic point of view. I believe that through this organismic outlook alone we shall come to embody the meaning of the neurosis in its true, impartial significance. In this conception we shall be in a position to view differentiation, under whatsoever form it manifests itself, as the fallacy of self-sufficiency, as the delusion of separateness that it is. . . . Only in this organismic outlook shall we come to understand the true significance of the neuroses in the sense of really encompassing the disharmony embodied in them. (*The Social Basis of Consciousness*, pp. 128-30.)

Some of the essays and stories published in *Mental Health* during the early years of the phylobiological investigations evidenced the sensing of this phylic behavior principle. The following sketches, exceptional in their inclusive trend, draw attention to the presence in man of this organic coordination —a coordination that is the biological heritage of the human race.

A LA MODE

It is probable that the most profound and searching truths are quite readily demonstrable to everyone if the person who voices them accepts them truly within his own life. After all, what is true is merely what is common to us all. There will be fewer words when there are fewer

of us denying this common root. In our widening diver-
gencies from a common principle of life we have tended
to substitute arbitrary sophistications of our own and,
in these misinterpretations, to *impose* values where values
would fall very naturally into their place among us, were
.we ourselves more at home with them. Life today has
become over-prescribed. We live by formulae. We doctor
and are doctored. Or if we do not prescribe we proscribe.
In either course, though, our program is external and
arbitrary. It does not express the natural feeling within
man's inherent life. Moreover, the recommendation of
yesterday is wholly abrogated tomorrow.

Said a friend of mine to me the other day—a woman I
have known for many years—"You know, the very latest
thing now is not to bathe. What one needs is not bathing
but rubbing with corn meal while standing in the sun and
breathing deeply!" I distinctly recall that just a very few
years ago this intrepid healer laid the source of all evil
to the eating of meat. Consistent with this doctrine she
stoutly maintained that there was no source of strength
to be found in all the world comparable to a diet of
lettuce. Indeed to her undaunted spirit lettuce seemed
in those days to represent nothing short of the millen-
nium. If she spoke, it was to lift her voice in a paean to
lettuce. Her world was attuned to leaves of grass and the
atmosphere about her was permeated with herbivorous
lyrics. But I recall a period still more remote in which
the secret of life for my friend lay in the deep muscles of
the spine, and whosoever would obtain perfect health it
was imperative for him that he spend his nights on the
bare floor. And yet I know of no one whose essential
feeling is more deeply sensitive to inherent human needs

than this same friend of mine notwithstanding her many diverse excursions into transient empiricisms.

Everyone remembers that at one time the panacea for all ills was sour milk. At still another the daily consumption of yeast cakes was the guarantee for long life and future prosperity. We all remember when Fletcherism held the boards, and today the physical culturists are still no less in the limelight. But I do not hesitate to say that in the *spirit* in which these different pharmaceutics are proffered they are no different from the beneficent nutmeg fervently recommended by the Negro mammy, or the amulets and herbs confided to our possession by the magic hands of the Indian medicine man. Empty talismans all of them! And yet beneath them all I do not doubt there is somehow felt the urge of a human need that requires sober consideration when it has come to be shared soberly among us.

It is the recognition of this common, inherent need that is my plea and along with it the giving to what is transient but a transient place, recognizing that it is but a temporary substitute that must await a deeper and more permanent solution. I think it is conceded that the cutting down of a meat diet has its undoubted value. For aught I know, people who advocate its entire elimination may be quite wise in recommending this course. But how does one know? How can anyone know as long as he merely accepts prescription from a basis of our widely divergent sophistications? It is this element of the extraneous, the transient and enforced, this element of interdiction, of repression, of substitution that is the rub. Undoubtedly people who eat or drink to excess are benefited by a proscriptive regime of diet but, after all, proscription is but a temporary expedient. In the attitude of mind that says "this is good for you" and "that is good for you," however necessary such injunctions may be as momentary safeguards, there is not the opportunity for the person to discover for himself what he feels to be his own inherent need. While the temporary value of interdiction cannot be denied, I think we shall come to see that it must ultimately be replaced by an attitude of mind so close to what are the inherent and common roots of our human needs that the individual will no longer require to be dominated as now by necessary interdictions upon his unhealthy choice. When, in short, we begin to study what are the organism's needs, mental and physical— when we shall have begun to search into the causes that underlie an excessive and improper use of food or drink, we shall see that there is some pain, some conflict that underlies these evidences of our human greed; that what is back of such ineptitudes is the obsessive effort to compensate within one sphere of life for what is the undoubted dearth of human satisfaction in another. When we have completely studied and synthesized our human needs, the individual and society will cease automatically to desire whatever is harmful to its organism.

In sum, with the intelligent recognition of man's common needs, there will come the intelligent inquiry into the practical means of fulfilling them. For repression, interdiction and injunction (however salutary to man in his present state of development) will become quite obsolete provisions in his economy when, sensing the common necessities of his living, man will realize the common source from which these necessities arise. In this day man will quite naturally welcome only what is contributory to the life of his organism because of its continuity with the organic needs of the race as a whole.

IN REVERSE

I wonder how many people have ever considered the possibility that they are defeating their own interests in the very actions through which they would promote them, that their efforts are opposed by equal counter-efforts, that their lives are actually geared in reverse the while they think they are proceeding in a forward course.

Hard pressed by its many incommodities we have vainly sought in all directions to discover a remedy for the outward signs of this condition, and in our unchecked quest we have not lacked theoretical formulations to account for this contradictory purpose within us. In our misdirected endeavors certain aspects of this anomaly have been ignorantly described in many quarters as neurasthenia, psychasthenia, chronic indigestion, dementia praecox, nervous prostration, hypochondriasis, arthritis, hysteria, enteroptosis, autointoxication, etc., etc., etc.; and the cause for these disorders, as set forth in the Greek, Latin and English languages, has been as variably assigned to "inherited weakness," congenital taint, high blood-pressure, indiscretions of diet, unrequited love, abscessed teeth, enlarged thyroid, a mother-complex, overwork or no work at all. And finally there has been the effort to trace the condition to the hidden presence of an undisclosed tragedy experienced in early infancy and prudently repressed!

Naturally, the treatment has been of a correspondingly diversified character: rest cure, a sea voyage, the interdiction of all meats and the substitution of lettuce and other

grasses, lavage, yeast cakes, massage, aspirin, cold baths,
New Thought, the daily dozen, Coué, social service and
the industrial arts.

In a word, for something remotely conceived to be the
matter the remedy has been something remotely conceived to be the cure. At one time mistaking the trouble
for a disorder of the physical structures and at another
time for a disorder within the mental sphere, medicine
applies in the one instance remedies calculated to restore
the bodily functions, and in another remedies presumed
to affect the individual within his mental preoccupations.
But in a narrow interpretation of "mental" and "physical"
neither sphere has anything whatsoever to do with the
organ that is really affected. For the difficulty is that this
reverse trend is one that has laid hold upon the innermost
mood of its victims, eliciting all their sympathy on the
side of its backward interest. Thus in its approach to the
study of this regressive reaction medicine has applied its
investigations, as it were, to the wrong organ. That is
why our many devices for counteracting this organic impasse within us are unavailing. That is why, in our misguided efforts of relief, this prevalent condition continues
to hold sway among us, and why its self-defeating ends
have all the while been encouraged most by those whom
they would most defeat.

When we have come to study the essential mood of
man we shall find that it resides within the relationships
of his organism regarded as a common social unit. We
shall find that in the presence or absence of a coordination
within the life of man as an integral social unit depends
the health or disharmony of his essential mood. Where
there is a response within the individual's feeling to this
innate social mood he is quickened to constructive activity

and health. Where there is a lack of such response within the individual to this organic social continuum he is inevitably a prey to the inhibitions that place an embargo upon all his activities and outlooks. Nervousness and insanity will come into a true scientific reckoning when man's organic place in the social scheme about him comes also into its due acknowledgment and we have come to recognize that his mood, whether alert and forward or depressed and reversed, is dependent upon his relationships with his fellows as interactive elements in a common social organism.

IN VAIN

In Oscar Wilde's list of books that are not to be read he includes "all books that try to prove anything." As sweeping as this indictment is, there is at the same time something that is quite intriguing about it. Wilde was not analytic. I doubt if he himself knew what was the element in all dissertation that so repelled him. Certainly no one was at greater pains to present a convincing array of proof in support of what he believed than Oscar Wilde. It could therefore hardly have been the mere presentation of evidence to which he objected. Besides, if one thinks of it, the whole purpose of any book, or of any intellectual process whatsoever, even that expressed in the most casual conversation, is somehow an endeavor to state a conviction or make evident a belief. One cannot even venture the surmise that it will probably rain today without at least implying the evidence which repeated observation and long experience furnish him in support of this apparently quite offhand view. Wilde was too intelligent not to have known this, even though he may never have formulated it in conscious terms. And so when he said what he did about books that try to prove anything, he must have had, if not in mind at least at heart, something very different from what he said or seemed to say.

The books which were so abhorrent to the soul of Wilde were not, after all, the books that prove anything but the books that *try* to prove anything. He had in mind books that present the obvious effort of the author to force convictions of his own upon his readers. Wilde disliked the furrowed brow and the perspiring palm. From this point of view there is a whole world of thought in this unqualified interdiction of Oscar Wilde's. The fact is that within the sphere of our human contacts people who *try* to do anything invariably have an ulterior object in view. Their object is always their own self-interest and the securing of the device best calculated to conceal the conflict within their own lives. It does not matter whether their efforts are directed toward the alleviation of the condition of the poor or whether toward prison reform, the uplift of humanity, the writing of good books, or the saving of the soul of their fellow man. Wheresoever they are proceeding upon a basis of private conviction and are *trying* to do something about it, they are, like the books cited by Oscar Wilde, people to be avoided.

The reason why prohibition is not a success and never will be is the element in it of trying to "put over" something—of struggling and fighting to enforce a principle. A true principle that is truly felt enforces itself. It is the principle we do not truly believe in that we struggle to enforce. The *principle* that underlies all the heated endeavor of the prohibitionists is perfectly true and sane. But it is not the principle which the prohibitionists have in mind when they try to enforce it. There is really more drinking today in this country as a result of prohibition than there has ever been before. Every prohibitionist knows this and in redoubling his efforts to quell this growing tide of alcoholism he knows very well that his efforts will but further swell this paradoxical result. Since the prohibitionist knows this, and yet proceeds with the policy of prohibition, it is clear that it is not prohibition that he really has in mind. It is clear that the principle submerges something very different and that this submerged element is a secret which the prohibitionist keeps to himself. The situation becomes simpler when we realize that the question is not what is the prohibitionist in particular endeavoring to do, but what are all people endeavoring to do who are endeavoring to enforce something.

The desire to prove is always the concealment of a private wish on the part of the individual as contrasted with the social gesture he offers in support of his proof. The man who wants privately to prove something or to do something by way of help to others is socially concealing the fact that he doubts his own proof and that he does not accept his own help. There is in him the obvious intention of the principle in question but also there is the submerged intention that underlies and contradicts the principle. This same division—the intention and the counter-intention—that is within him he must perforce through his social gesture inculcate in others. The up-lifters and the propagandists are really hiding something and they must of necessity exert their influence toward inducing others to hide something too. What the prohibitionists want, of course unconsciously, is nothing different from what the advocates of segregation in the red light district wanted. The purpose of both is no other than the concealment of their own conflict. Prohibitionists the world over, whether of alcohol or venery or what not, want one and the same thing—namely, that this thing of division, that this canker of concealment and of pretense within themselves, shall also spread to the bosoms of others and give social support to their own private concealment and repression.

This element of private concealment that exists socially under the disguise of spurious proof, argument and uplift is so general that we are blind to our own dilemma. The platitudes of such adept literary magicians as Oscar Wilde or Bernard Shaw are, in their symbolic way, not far of the mark. The gestures they travesty in the pages of books are like the gestures of people in their social expressions. In place of the actual, organic expression of a true principle truly believed, such books, like people and their blue laws, represent the substitutions and concealments that try to prove something or force a conviction upon the lives of other people. People who try to prove anything are necessarily a bore, and a bore never helped anybody but himself. That is what a bore is out for—the satisfaction for himself that is derived through the penalty he imposes on other people, through the contrasts he implies between himself and other people in his very effort to help them. Poets and children are never bores. That is because they never try to help anybody.

Our helpfulness, like our proofs, is based upon an attitude of differentiation within our social life. The only beneficence that may flow from one man to another is in the giving of himself through the realization of their common identity. In this there is no thought of helpfulness, there is no thesis to be proved. We need to recognize that our private interests and differentiations are the real instigators of whatever so-called helpfulness we offer and of whatever proofs we attempt to enforce.

On the delectable day when there comes to us this realization there will be less of these self-conscious and self-righteous substitutions doing service for the private individual, and in the healthy concourse of all individuals upon a common basis of understanding and participation through their common rights all of our beneficent enterprises will be clearly seen to be but a social much ado about nothing.

Although the thesis of the phylic solidarity of man's intrinsic consciousness is naturally not developed in these short pieces, they contain such significant phrases as "a common principle of life," "the organic needs of the race as a whole," "coordination within the life of man as an integral social unit," "common social organism," and "a common basis of understanding and participation." But more important than the phrases is the mood or feeling-background from which the three essays were written—a mood or feeling that is expressive of "an organic social continuum."

In Chapter III we saw that our emotional or affective conditioning in childhood tends to isolate each individual, cutting him off from common feeling-participation with others of his kind. We saw that each individual comes to behave as a divisive, self-centered unit of motivation. The "normal" or habitual frame of reference in the field of man's behavior is thus necessarily alien to the biologically inclusive perspective of phylobiology. In his armor-plated aloofness the individual does not want to accept a point of view that seems to him to repudiate his very self. He is prone to interpret it as either mystical or abstruse. Because of the automatism of his separative conditioning, he tends to turn aside with the comment, "I just can't understand." This attitude was certainly common enough among the students who wrote the sketches in this volume.

Examined objectively, free from the haze of affect that ordinarily blinds us, the principle of the phylo-organism is neither abstruse nor mystical. It is a principle as intrinsic to man's organism as the principle of physical growth. We are familiar with the strong urge toward health and coordination of function within the physiology of the single individual. This urge is no less strong and positive in respect to the health of man as a solidaric species once he has dealt with the blighting circumstance of his social neurosis.

These formulations in regard to the social neurosis and the essentially phylic nature of man's feeling and motivation were developed by Dr. Burrow as a result of his study of the immediate interrelational behavior of man as this behavior occurred within his own organism in an experimental-group setting. They were forged in the laboratory of human behavior. It may be mentioned, however, that recent developments in many other fields of scientific endeavor offer evidence which is not without interest for a phylobiological orientation. Today, investigators in many diverse spheres of research recognize that the whole is something more than the sum of its parts. They recognize that the organismic interfunctioning among the parts and the emergent properties of the whole must be studied if the phenomena are to be rightly understood and basic principles formulated. The present tendency in biology and anthropology, in such fields as child development and animal behavior, is in the direction of focusing increasing interest on the factor of functional continuity, on the interrelation of parts and on the primary significance of the whole. The significance of the individual element is correspondingly modified.

In *Mutual Aid* Kropotkin sounded the note that was to bring the newer orientation to the study of animal groups. This early observer stressed the significant role of social interdependence and cooperation in many animal species. His frequent illustrations indicate that mutual aid is the rule rather than the exception throughout the animal kingdom, and he mentions the little-recognized fact that Darwin emphasized the significance of social coordination in the survival of the fittest. It becomes increasingly clear that the common tendency among people to look to Darwinian concepts for justification of ruthlessly aggressive and competitive trends involves a misreading of this gifted originator of the doctrine of evolution.

But the resistance to the viewpoint first advanced by Kropotkin in 1890 was so great that the writings of this pioneer student of animal aggregations were largely disregarded. It is only recently that such eminent biologists as Allee, Emerson, Wheeler, and others have verified and extended Kropotkin's observations on the principle of behavioral cohesion among animals. Allee has studied the matter intensively under experimentally controlled conditions, and concludes that communal life is the normal and universal condition among animal species, that all animals are immersed in some society, and that a social medium is necessary for the conservation and renewal of life among them. He says:*

> Evidently mutual interdependence, or automatic cooperation, is sufficiently widespread among the animal kingdom to warrant the conclusion given above that it ranks as one of the fundamental qualities of animal protoplasm, and probably of protoplasm in general.

Other modern students of ecology have shown that in-

---

* W. C. Allee, *Animal Aggregations: A Study in General Sociology* (Chicago: University of Chicago Press, 1931), p. 357. Quoted by permission of the publisher.

terdependence exists not only within animal groups but is characteristic of the life process of plants as well, and of the interrelationship of plants and animals.

Coming closer to man from the point of view of evolutionary development, Yerkes and Köhler point out that the primates in general, particularly chimpanzees, habitually live in social groups and that the bonds which unite the individuals are a very real force. When a chimpanzee is separated from his accustomed group his first and strongest drive is to be reunited with it. Enforced separation from their kind causes chimpanzees to be fearful, to rage, to lose appetite, to become ill, and even to die. They will literally risk their lives to get back to their group.

Biologically, man is no less dependent on his group. Anthropologists tell us that our primitive forbears survived because of their capacity for concord and cooperation. For instance, Sir Arthur Keith stresses coordination within the group as the important factor in human survival. Careful studies show that organized warfare came relatively late in man's cultural development, that a militant and competitive instinct is not native to the human race. In this connection, the following quotation from Clyde Kluckhohn's *Mirror for Man* is interesting:*

It is not certain that warfare existed during the Old Stone Age. The indications are that it was unknown during the earlier part of the New Stone Age in Europe and the Orient. Settlements lack structures that would have defended them against attack. Weapons seem to be limited to those used in hunting animals. Some promi-

---

* Clyde Kluckhohn, *Mirror for Man—the Relation of Anthropology to Modern Life* (New York: McGraw-Hill Book Co., 1949), p. 55. Quoted by permission of the publisher.

nent ethnologists read the record of more recent times to mean that war is not endemic but a perversion of human nature. Organized, offensive warfare was unknown in aboriginal Australia. Certain areas of the New World seem to have been completely free from war in the pre-European period.

In his book *On Being Human*, Ashley Montagu gathers together much telling evidence to indicate the force of the cooperative urge throughout the evolutionary development of modern man.*

Observers of still-existing primitive tribes report a group cohesion and rapport which has been largely lost in sophisticated "civilized" societies. In *Instinct and the Unconscious* W. H. R. Rivers presents instances showing that common understanding and mutual aid are inherent features of the daily activity of primitive tribes. He stresses the coordination and social solidarity of these groups and the remarkable lack of personalism and competition. Kropotkin makes these significant observations of a primitive social group:**

> I remember how vainly I tried to make some of my Tungus friends understand our civilization of individualism; they could not. . . . The fact is that a savage, brought up in ideas of a tribal solidarity in everything . . . is as incapable of understanding a "moral" European, who knows nothing of that solidarity, as the average European is incapable of understanding the savage. . . . Wherever we go we find the same sociable manners, the same spirit of solidarity. . . . The primitive man . . . identifies his

---

* Ashley Montague, *On Being Human* (New York: Henry Schuman, Inc., 1950).

** P. Kropotkin, *Mutual Aid—A Factor of Evolution* (New York: Alfred A. Knopf, 1920), pp. 83–88. Quoted by permission of the publisher.

own existence with that of his tribe; and without that
quality mankind never would have attained the level it
has attained now.

In our commonplace everyday life this principle of solidarity seems to be completely submerged in the incessant,
ruthless competition rampant among civilized men. It is
dissipated and nullified by the social neurosis. However, the
capacity for inclusive feeling is still there. Dr. Burrow makes
this point clear in his *Social Basis of Consciousness.* He says:*

It is commonly taught by the schoolmen that self-
preservation is the first law of nature. I do not believe it.
I believe that the instinct of tribal preservation is by far
the dominant urge among us. I believe that this instinct
takes precedence over the impulse of self-maintenance to
a degree that renders individual life insignificant in comparison. In face of the reflex assertion of the impulse of
race-preservation the individual is brushed heedlessly aside.
A group of miners will without thought descend one after
another into a gas-filled chamber to rescue a fellow-
workman from death and one after another share the fate
of their comrade. We all know countless instances of
this rescue-impulse as a response to the organic instinct of
race unity. Nor is it confined to these more sensational
expressions of the impulse. The scientist in his laboratory
toiling daily with indefatigable energy, receiving usually
a remuneration that is not adequate to his actual needs
and too often without even the sympathetic appreciation
on the part of his environment of the significance of his
quest, as it relates to the communal need he would serve,

---

* Trigant Burrow, *The Social Basis of Consciousness—A Study in Organic
Psychology* (New York: Harcourt, Brace & Co., 1927), pp. 127–28. Quoted
by permission of the publisher.

expresses equally this same organic instinct of racial solidarity.

Strange as it may seem, the common presence of grave danger and of imminent death fosters the renewal of the primordial bond among human beings. Expressions of the strong feeling uniting mankind appear conspicuously in combat. We are all familiar with the countless occasions when men in the front lines have spontaneously sacrificed their lives for the welfare of their buddies and the group. More telling perhaps in revealing the common bond of humanity are the numerous authenticated instances reported during World War II where the urge to mutual aid transcended the lines of battle —the Nazi pilot saved from drowning by a Jewish soldier of the British army who swam to the aid of the German and held him up until help came; the Canadian pilot who dropped his indispensable dinghy to the German airman he had shot down into the sea; the German infantryman who, with his own body, shielded a wounded Russian prisoner of war whom his comrades would have killed. These and innumerable other evidences of a sense of unity too deep for destruction have marked man's course since the first years of recorded history.

Recent investigations in the field of child development also lend support to Dr. Burrow's phylo-organismic thesis. Earlier writers on the subject had assumed that the child was by nature individualistic and asocial, and they concentrated on the control of competitive and destructive trends. Many modern students, however, recognize the extent to which these earlier interpretations were biased by the competitive, highly individualized culture in which we live today. Current researches disclose that the primary impulse of children in the early years of life is toward cooperation rather than aggressive striving. Competitive behavior is generally lacking until about the third year of life, after which time it occurs with increasing frequency. Vigotsky presents experimental data to support the view that the child's language and other higher psychological functions originate as forms of cooperative activity and that egocentric tendencies do not develop until later. Various studies have shown that the young child is generous by nature; that he has no sense of personal property, of things belonging exclusively to himself. In this connection, Kurt Lewin makes these significant remarks:

> The child, to a greater extent than the adult, is a *dynamic unity*. . . . The "I" or self is only gradually formed, perhaps in the second or third year. Not until then does the concept of property appear, of the belonging of a thing to his own person. ("Environmental Forces," in *Handbook of Child Psychology*, edited by Carl Murchison, Clark University Press, 1933, p. 619.)

The inclusive feeling on the part of children that disavows personal ownership is often met with misunderstanding by adults trained to possessiveness and a me-versus-you dichotomy. A recent newspaper contains an account of a three-year-old boy who was severely punished for distributing throughout the neighborhood the packages found beneath his Christmas tree. In her lack of sympathy with the child's native generosity, the mother reflected an impairment in feeling that exists throughout mankind. She was training her boy to conform to the social formula, to hold tight to what is "one's own." For her, as for all of us, generosity is for *ours* and against *others*. This is the habitual mood to which the incoming generation is conditioned. Self-centered reactions make up the "I"-persona, the pseudo-identity which the child is henceforth trained to impose upon his organism; and little short of a threat to life itself will reveal the latent but ever-present sense of unity binding together the elements of the species.

As Dr. Burrow points out, man's great need is to bring to maturity this principle of identity and coordination native to his organism. Today, the group cannot be less than the entire community of mankind. All the peoples of the earth are inseparably bound into a global whole, and only a phylic pattern of consciousness can encompass the global nature of our life.

Recently a panel of scientists representing various disciplines and countries, and working under the auspices of UNESCO, made a strong statement in regard to the biological solidarity of mankind:

> Biological studies lend support to the ethic of universal brotherhood. . . . Man is born a social being who can reach his full development only through interaction with his fellows. The denial at any point of this social bond between men and man brings with it disintegration. In this sense, every man is his brother's keeper. For every man is a piece of the continent, a part of the main, because he is involved in mankind. (*United Nations Reporter*, September 10, 1950.)

There is increasing objective evidence of a basic principle of cohesion underlying human behavior. But we must squarely face the fact of our subjective hostility to such a thesis. It does violence to our treasured beliefs, our wishful fancies and our cherished presuppositions; it runs counter to our deeply ingrained ideas of independent self-sufficiency, "free competition," and "rugged individualism." We must recognize that the separative, wishful mood to which we were conditioned in the nursery is the chief obstacle to a clear recognition of the unitary basis of man's social motivation and behavior. Phylobiology makes explicit that there is a principle of coordination primarily activating the interrelational behavior of man. This principle rests on firm biological ground and possesses in no sense religious, sentimental, or mystical connotations. It is the natural balance-wheel governing man's basic motivation. The behavior of the individual can be sane and effective only when it is in accord with this biosocial principle.

CHAPTER IX

Tensional Patterns and Man's Behavior

The biosocial disorganization of mankind is inextricably associated with a conflict between physiological patterns of response. This is one of the most outstanding discoveries of phylobiology. Dr. Burrow's researches show that the free-functioning physiology of man's organism as it relates him to his environment is today hindered and restricted. They show that, along with the artificial separation in feeling of the individuals of the race, there has occurred a specific interference within the physiological processes of the individual. Both these phenomena are aspects of the functional *faux pas* in man's development to which we referred earlier—the *faux pas* connected with the attempt to mediate feeling-processes through the restricted avenues of image- and symbol-projection.

In its native function, feeling is the complete engagement of the total organism. Feeling is unitary and whole, both within the individual and within the species. Healthy feeling is an expression of man, not of "me"; it is an expression of the total organism, not of the head and the symbol. But, as we saw in Chapter III, man's feeling-processes have become largely displaced into the head. Man now tries to project his feeling in the same way that he projects his symbols and his ideas. In this process feeling has become curtailed; it has become distorted into partitive ("me-first") feeling or affect. Communication now is from part-brain to part-brain. It is not from whole organism to whole organism. The part of the brain that has the capacity to deal with symbols does not now relate men to one another directly and objectively.

As Dr. Burrows says in *The Neurosis of Man* (1949):*

> This cerebral part-function or segment now relates individuals only vicariously to one another, as it also relates them for the most part only vicariously to the environment. . . . This part-function represented by the "I"-persona with its autopathic feeling, or affect, has thrust itself between the organism and its environment. With the recognition of this socio-symbolic segment or partitive function of the brain, my associates and I found ourselves faced with a problem in neurophysiology. As this cerebral process of symbol-formation relates not only the organism of the individual but also the organism of the species to the environment, our problem—as ultimately every medical problem—became a phylic as well as a physiological one. This finding and its organismic significance in relation to human behavior pointed to a new field of investigation as well as to a new method of investigating it.

Dr. Burrow's intensive experiments in the behavior of social groups—groups composed, as we have said, of the so-called

---

* *The Neurosis of Man—An Introduction to a Science of Human Behavior* (New York: Harcourt, Brace & Co., 1949), p. 184. Quoted by permission of the publisher.

normal and the frankly neurotic, of rich and poor, of psychiatrists and laymen—disclosed the presence in man of a
restricted pattern of physiological tension, and indicated that
this tensional pattern was associated with a partitive type of
brain-function. There is evidence that this biologically
anomalous functioning of the brain in relating man to his
fellows, and its concomitant pattern of physiological tensions,
is the direct cause of false social perceptions, of interrelational
prejudice and behavioral conflict. Where it is a question of
the faulty functioning of any other organ, say the stomach or
the kidney, we feel the pain and strain resulting from the
malfunction within our own organism. But, as we shall see,
where it is a question of dysfunction in the brain, connected
with the projection of affect, we project the strain and pain
along with the affect. We localize *in others* the pain that is
actually *within our own tissues*.

In Chapter III we indicated that man's relationship with
his environment, both physical and social, is largely mediated
by the function of attention. It was on this function that
later phases of the phylobiological researches centered. Here,
it was thought, might be a clue to the disruption of the
balance of function uniting man to his fellows. As we know,
attention is not merely an abstract or symbolic process.
Physiological components play a prominent role in any act of
attention. For example, when one is startled by a sudden, in-
explicable noise, the organism attends to the situation
physiologically. The muscles of the spine stiffen, the head is
raised, the ear grows keen, the eyes search the surroundings,
and the heart beats faster in order to send more blood to every
part of the body in readiness for a possible emergency. This is,
of course, an unusual situation; but every act of attention,
however commonplace, involves similar bodily changes, al-

though perhaps less noticeably. It is inevitable that any dysfunction in the attentional process has its physiological
counterpart.

The physiological components underlying man's disordered
feeling and attention came to the fore as group analysis progressed. For the consistent challenge and frustration of socially
accepted affect-projections, as well as those which were
patently neurotic, tended to throw the organism back upon its
neglected physiological sensations. In consequence, the students were given an opportunity to withdraw their attention
from projective focusing on the behavior of others and to
direct it instead upon strains and tensions internal to their own
organisms. This was a most important step in coming to grips
with the common factors responsible for our manifold, interrelational conflicts.

Words are curious things. On the one hand they can
illumine a dark void and make it live. On the other, they can
prove to be mere will-o'-the-wisps leading us into a bog of
misunderstanding. The lines in the previous paragraph sound
clear and simple enough. But they describe an approach that
is so radically different from any that has been attempted in
the field of human behavior, that the reader has no basis from
which to evaluate them and may well be led astray by an
effort to read into them concepts that are familiar to him.

"The consistent challenge and frustration of affect-projections"—what do these words mean in terms of phylobiology?
Let us say, first, that one's habitual tendency is to project upon
others the cause of one's disordered feeling, or affect. Irritation, for instance, may occur at any time, and always seems to
result from something that has happened outside one's organism—the rudeness of a salesgirl, perhaps, lack of appreciation on the part of an associate, a critical attitude in one's
friends or family. One's efforts to relieve the irritation are

reflexly directed toward changing the behavior of the other fellow. This customary reaction in our interrelational life is identical with that of a man who stumbles over a stool and then curses or kicks it. Although recourse to outside adjustment is unavailing, such affect-projection is socially accepted as bona fide. In our accustomed social interchange each of us is subjectively involved in affect; we do not observe it objectively.

If one is to observe affect, the first task is to block its projection. It is essential that we first negate the all-compelling urge to look to the behavior of others to explain one's hostile or aggressive moods. It is essential that we cease to blame others for the disordered affective response resident within our own organisms. Dr. Burrow devoted years to the study of affect, not *out there* but *within himself in a group setting*—within the physiology of his own tissues. He recognized that he was an organismic part of the material he studied; that the affect-distortions he observed were common to mankind on our present level of behavioral adaptation, and that no one could in any valid sense *look at* these distortions as though they were discrete phenomena occurring in another person. In other words, Dr. Burrow was observing behavior within himself at the same time that he was observing it within the group. This is of the nature of species-solidarity. And it was this inclusive basis of feeling that made possible the consistent challenge and frustration of habitual affect-involvements.

Prolonged self-training in directing the attention inward to the physiological strain and conflict underlying affect-projection gradually led to increased facility in discriminating patterns of tensional response. It led to the internal differentiation of two contrasting tensional patterns, each of which was related to a specific type of behavioral adjustment. In one pattern, the tensions were concentrated about the eyes and in the forepart of the head. The behavior accompanying this pattern was laden with affect and prejudice; it was wishful, self-centered, of a dualistic and partitive nature. When this pattern is in operation the individual expresses the neurosis of man. This mode of adjustment with its concomitant pattern of physiological tensions Dr. Burrow called *ditention*. In the other pattern, tensions were not predominantly localized within the symbolic segment. There was a sensation of relaxation in this area, and the tensions were more generally distributed throughout the organism as a whole. It was observed that when this tensional pattern was present there was no longer the compulsion to project one's affect, to blame the other person, to get even with someone, to be prejudiced in one's feeling and outlook. The projected affect with its partitive physiology had been reabsorbed within the total pattern of feeling and physiology native to man as a biological species. The behavior accompanying this pattern of tension was direct, unprejudiced, and oriented to the welfare of mankind rather than to the private-profit motive of the "I"-persona. It resulted in unitary and balanced social relations. This behavioral mode and its accompanying neuromuscular pattern Dr. Burrow called *cotention*.

Dr. Burrow early noticed that, with himself, the cotentive pattern was invariably accompanied by a slowing of the breathing rate. This was a very striking observation, since breathing plays a vital role in the physiological and psychological processes of the human organism. It led to an extensive series of instrumental studies of physiological reactions within himself and his associates to record whatever functional characteristics might differentiate the two patterns. It was found that the physiology of the organism differed in cotention and ditention in the following ways: There was a marked slowing of the rate of breathing in cotention, and at the same time the breathing became noticeably deeper. There was a consistent decrease in number and extent of eye-movements during cotention. This was true whether the subject being tested was focusing his eyes upon a given point or was using them to look at objects or pictures. In cotention the subject perceived visual objects more as a whole; there was less focusing on individual parts or items. There was a definite alteration in brain-wave patterns during cotention. This alteration consisted in a decrease in the amount of alpha rhythm and a reduction of the amplitude of the alpha waves. These changes could be demonstrated not only when the subject was lying down with eyes closed but also when he was actively engaged in such tasks as reading or mental arithmetic.*

It is always difficult to bridge the gap from old to new concepts. Recognition of the significance of physiological patterns of tension in relation to man's behavior will prove no exception. Without definite internal observation of these patterns, one is handicapped in his understanding of cotention as it relates man to his fellows, and of the technique for re-establishing this organismic mode of behavior. While analogies are never entirely satisfactory, they can be helpful in communicating new meanings. Dr. Burrow has mentioned that a fairly good analogy can be drawn between the discipline involved in cotention and the discipline necessary for the acquirement of a physical skill. Say you are a tennis player and have a faulty stroke. The physiological elements of the faulty stroke are faulty patterns of muscular tension. The defective organization and coordination of these patterns results in the inadequate stroke. These neuromuscular patterns, however, have now become habitual with you on the tennis court. They feel "right" to you and you constantly slip back into your muscular errors although you may be mentally concentrating

---

* Instrumental recordings in respect to ditention and cotention are fully reported in the Appendix to *The Neurosis of Man*.

on overcoming your awkwardness. Every athlete is familiar
with this experience. What the tennis instructor does is to
instill in his pupil the muscular "feel" of the correct stroke.
He places the racquet correctly in the student's hand, moves
his arm through the proper swing, indicates the most effective
stance for balance and movement. The pupil's task is to
acquire through repeated practice the physiological sense of
the awkwardness of his habitual stroke and to build up a
muscular sense of the coordinated tensional pattern that underlies correct stroking. One cannot be a consistently good tennis
player until this internal sense of the faulty and the correct
stroke is established. Once it is established, one can forget
such worries and preoccupations as to whether the ball is going
out of court or into the net. When the muscular "feel" is
right, the stroke is correct and the ball will inevitably follow
the desired course.

It is similar with ditention and cotention. Because of our
social conditioning from infancy, the physiological pattern of
faulty attention, or ditention, is now habitual to man. This
pattern feels natural and "right," although it leads to various
forms of disordered social behavior. Our task, like that of the
tennis player, is twofold. First, one has to get a physiological
"feel" of the awkwardness of this tensional pattern as it
determines our social behavior. And second, it is necessary
to establish a physiological sense of the cotentive pattern. As
with a sound tennis stroke, the acquirement of cotention
entails drill and discipline. And just as the drill and discipline
required in tennis can be applied only on the tennis court, so
the drill and discipline that thwarts ditention and re-establishes
cotention must be applied in an actual social setting. When
the phylobiological student has acquired the "feel" of the
physiological pattern accompanying cotention, he is assured
of his biologically and socially healthy response. He need no

longer concern himself with such projective and inconsistent evaluations as "good" and "bad," "love" and "hate," and the thousand and one other behavioral dichotomies characterizing our normal social life.

It will be readily understood that the inertia and resistance one encounters in such a relatively simple adjustment as correcting a poor tennis stroke are markedly intensified where there is an effort to correct a behavioral pattern that has become systematized throughout society. We are all reflexly in favor of our partitive feeling and our partitive physiology. Our training since infancy has been overwhelmingly in this direction. Generations of mankind have lived predominantly on this superficial level. So that the physiological training involved in blocking one's habitual ditentive behavior and restoring the organism's cotentive balance is in a very real sense a re-conditioning. It is the recovery of man's native pattern of organismic wholeness—a pattern that provides us with a reliable norm for the evaluation of human behavior.

In his last published paper, Dr. Burrow says:

> Cotention is the primary pattern that characterizes the spontaneous behavior of the infant in relation to its environment. This cotentive principle is also operative in the balanced process of integration that characterizes the disinterested mentation of the scientist in his approach to his material of observation and analysis. Indeed, what the child has by nature and the scientist by training, all mankind possesses potentially in the primary unity and integrity of his total organism's relation to its environment. Cotention is man's biological staple; as much so as food or air or soil. ("Prescription for Peace," in *Explorations in Altruistic Love and Behavior*, edited by Pitirim A. Sorokin, Beacon Press, 1950, p. 110.)

There is nothing esoteric or impractical about cotention. Everything else is impractical. Everything else is awkwardness, lack of rapport, absorption in behavioral disorder. Cotention insures total participation with one's objective environment and with one's fellows. It represents the norm of health in the field of man's social behavior. Cotention is as practical as health is practical. It is as practical as the direct behavior of the child, as the attitude of the trained scientist when at work in his laboratory. On our present basis man's behavior is wasteful and inefficient. The projection of affect, the hostility and antagonism, the lack of communication among people is highly impractical. Because of the universal systematization of a̤ ̤ ̤t and the corresponding development of a false personality, or "I"-persona, ditentive man makes no real contact with his human environment. Cotention makes contact and communication possible. It makes possible the common adoption of basic measures for meeting man's worldwide conflict and dissension.

The observation of internal tensional patter... brings the problem of man's behavior out of the realm of discussion and verbal suasion, and into the world of objective observation and demonstrable experience. The reactivation of the cotentive pattern is in itself not difficult. It does not entail effort or striving in the usual sense. Cotention is a matter of observing objectively our internal subjective processes—a matter of *feeling* the ditentive reaction as the severe impediment it is to the organism's natural balance of function. It is ditention that is the rub. It is our social involvement in the inept mode of ditention that is the chief obstruction to cotention and to functional coordination with our fellows.

Man urgently needs to adopt an organismic view of human behavior. In this view emphasis is placed upon mankind and not upon the isolated individual. Just as the physiology of the growing organism is an expanding total process, so the behavior of man developed from the total pattern of feeling or motivation of the group or species. But in our life today man's solidarity of feeling is overlaid with private affect; our biological verity is obscured beneath our partitive ("me-first") conditioning. No matter what ideology he lives under, the individual today is not free. He pays universal obeisance to a system of morality that is completely devoid of biological values. He does not lead a full or balanced life. He is a slave to social images. He is ruled by traditional prejudices, completely subservient to the complex of affects making up his false personality, or "I"-persona. Man cannot be free until the principle of species solidarity is reinstated throughout his feeling-processes. And that does not mean that all people will be alike. There is variation, not monotony, throughout nature—there is difference without conflict. The re-establishment of cotention will enormously enhance true individuality. But it must be emphasized that cotention is a mode of behavior belonging to man as a race or species, and that it is only as it is regained by him in this community sense that it can become truly effective. Only then will balanced function be re-established in the field of man's sociobiological interrelations.

In his fantasy, *Through the Looking-Glass*, Lewis Carroll describes the complicated and utterly fatuous preparations of Tweedledum and Tweedledee for a tremendous conflict over a rattle—a fight that they abandon with alacrity when they are frightened by a big black crow. Lewis Carroll may or may not have been a satirist with an intuitive perception of human frailties. But his ludicrous account of the two brothers, bitterly complaining about their aches and pains while they collect quantities of articles with which to arm themselves, gravely insisting all the while that they will fight, that they *must* fight

—at least till dinner—is a painfully accurate picture of the external aspect of man's present behavioral situation.

The Tweedledum-Tweedledee pattern is familiar to us all. It is the pattern of the "I"-persona. The "I"-persona is forever going to extreme lengths to prepare for hostilities that grow out of an infantile mood. By turns aggressive and timid, but continually preoccupied with his own prestige, man is impelled to fight by an obsessive urge he has never tried to understand. A phylo-organismic interpretation of behavioral conflict demands that we abandon the solemn farce of all Tweedledums and Tweedledees and adopt an immediate, internal, societal approach to man's disordered behavior. It demands that we turn aside from the fascination of this or that external circumstance, this or that moral judgment, and face human conflict as a problem internal to ourselves as a race or species. In this course we shall greatly simplify our lives, both as individuals and as communities. We shall set aside partitive, wishful thinking based on affect, and resolve the seemingly hopeless impasse in which ditention has today involved us.

"Absorbed as we constantly are in affects and pretensions," says Dr. Burrow, "our life has become a vast social charade. With our prejudices, our projections and our obsessive conflicts, we are but tilting at windmills. Dwelling from day to vicarious day in a fanciful medium of wishful incitements, the world of Little Man is but a bauble shop; his partitive debates, his political wranglings, but the fuss and feathers of an empty pageant. His military battles but the conquest of tin soldiers. His wars with all their bloodshed and horror but make-believe toy wars. Man needs to stand on his own feet. He needs to come to himself." (Unpublished.)

Index of Sketches